sushi

sushi

easy recipes for making sushi at home

Emi Kazuko, Fiona Smith, Elsa Petersen-Schepelern

RYLAND

PETERS

& SMALL

LONDON NEW YORK

First published in the USA in 2006 by
Ryland Peters & Small, Inc.
519 Broadway, 5th Floor
New York, NY 10012

10 9 8 7 6 5 4 3 2 1

Library of Congress Cataloging-in-Publication Data

Kazuko, Emi.
  Sushi : easy recipes for making sushi at home /
Emi Kazuko, Fiona Smith, Elsa Petersen-Schepelern.
     p. cm.
  Selected recipes from the author's books.
  Includes index.
  ISBN-13: 978-1-84597-097-0 (13-digit)
  ISBN-10: 1-84597-097-7 (10-digit)
  1. Cookery (Fish) 2. Sushi. I. Smith, Fiona. II.
Petersen-Schepelern, Elsa. III. Title.
TX747.K396 2005
641.6'92--dc22

                              2005016335

Printed in China

Designer Luana Gobbo
Commissioning Editor
  Elsa Petersen-Schepelern
Editor Susan Stuck
Production Gavin Bradshaw
Picture Research Tracy Ogino
Art Director Anne-Marie Bulat
Editorial Director Julia Charles

Food Stylists Emi Kazuko, Lucie McKelvie,
  Sunil Vijayakar, Linda Tubby
Prop Stylists Wei Tang, Hélène Lesur,
  Mary Norden

Notes
• All spoon measurements are level unless
otherwise noted.
• Eggs are medium unless otherwise specified. Raw
fish or shellfish and uncooked or partially cooked
eggs should not be served to the very old, frail,
young children, pregnant women, or those with
compromised immune systems.

contents

introduction

Sushi has come a long way in a relatively short time. It is amazing to think how the mystique surrounding this style of food kept it from being a favorite of home cooks for so long.

But how things have changed! Fresh sushi can be found everywhere from restaurants to supermarkets and fast-food outlets. It is served at elegant parties and the simplest home gatherings. Travel-weary tourists choose sushi restaurants for comforting, familiar food. Children have it in their lunchboxes, and even some school cafeterias serve it. Sushi has become this generation's healthy convenience food.

Techniques used in making sushi can be simplified for the home cook. One of the most popular styles, rolled sushi (*maki-zushi*), is easy and fun to make at home and, as soon as the process of rolling the rice has been mastered, a world of filling options becomes available. These days, our supermarkets are full of all kinds of sushi ingredients.

SUSHI-MAKING UTENSILS AND INGREDIENTS

Special sushi-making utensils and authentic ingredients are beautiful and useful, and sold even in supermarkets. Many brands of nori come pretoasted and in a variety of grades—use the best you can.

Some of the recipes in this book call for only half a sheet. When this is so, cut the sheets in half from the shortest side, so you are left with the most width. When making rolled sushi remember that rice is easier to handle with wet hands and nori is better to handle with dry. Keep a bowl of vinegared water and a towel on hand to make the job easier.

SERVING SUSHI

Traditional accompaniments for sushi are soy sauce, wasabi, and pickled ginger, often served with miso soup. A smear of wasabi can elevate a piece of sushi from the ordinary to something extraordinary.

If you do not want to add it in the sushi, serve a small pile on the side, or serve the sushi with a small dish of plain soy and one of wasabi and soy mixed together. Bought wasabi varies immensely; it is possible to find paste with a high percentage of real wasabi, but many are mostly horseradish—once again, buy the best you can or make your own (page 124).

Sushi is traditionally served immediately, but if you have to keep it for a while, wrap uncut rolls in plastic wrap. Keep in a cool place, but NOT in the refrigerator, which will make the rice hard and unpleasant—the vinegar in the rice will help preserve it for a short time.

ingredients

shoyu
(Japanese soy sauce)

mirin
*(Japanese sweet
rice wine, for
cooking only)*

su
*(Japanese
rice vinegar)*

sake
*(Japanese
rice wine)*

nori
(sheets of dried seaweed)

kanpyo
(dried gourd ribbons)

kombu
*(dried kelp for
cooking rice)*

white sesame seeds

black
sesame seeds

renkon, sliced
(lotus root)

shiso leaf
*(Japanese herb, also
known as perilla)*

Japanese ingredients are becoming more widely available in supermarkets and specialty food stores, but can certainly be found in Asian markets. This directory will help you identify them.

abura-age
(fried bean curd)

takuan
(pickled daikon radish)

fresh ginger

Japanese short-grained rice

umeboshi
(pickled red plums)

ready-made pickled ginger

wasabi paste
(also available as powder in cans)

shiitake
(dried mushrooms, also available fresh)

Sushi is a general term for all food with "sumeshi," or vinegared rice. Remember—sushi should never be put in the refrigerator (it will go hard.) The vinegar will help preserve it for a few days if kept, wrapped, in a cool place, such as a shady windowsill. To make sushi rice, boil 15 percent more water than rice. Don't take the lid off during cooking, or you will spoil the rice.

vinegared rice sumeshi

1¾ cups Japanese-style short-grained rice

1 piece of dried kelp (kombu), 2 inches square, for flavoring (optional)

3 tablespoons Japanese rice vinegar

2½ tablespoons sugar

2 teaspoons sea salt

MAKES 4 CUPS

1 Put the rice in a large bowl and wash it thoroughly, changing the water several times, until the water is clear. Drain and leave in the strainer for 1 hour. If short of time, soak the rice in clear, cold water for 10–15 minutes, then drain.

2 Transfer to a deep, heavy saucepan, add 2 cups water and a piece of dried kelp (kombu), if using. Cover and bring to a boil over high heat, about 5 minutes. Discard the kelp.

3 Lower the heat and simmer, covered, for about 10 minutes, or until all the water has been absorbed. Do not lift the lid until the end. Remove from the heat and leave, still covered, for about 10–15 minutes.

4 Mix the rice vinegar, sugar, and salt in a small glass measuring cup and stir until dissolved.

5 Transfer the cooked rice to a large, shallow dish or handai (Japanese wooden sumeshi tub). Sprinkle generously with the vinegar dressing.

6 Using a wooden spatula or spoon, fold the vinegar dressing into the rice. Do not stir. While folding, cool the rice quickly using a fan. Let the rice cool to body temperature before using to make sushi.

SUSHI ROLLS

Wonderful party food, nori rolls (*norimaki*) are probably the best-known sushi of all. A sheet of nori seaweed is spread with vinegared rice, a line of filling put down the middle, then the sheet is rolled up into a cylinder. The cylinder is cut into sections before serving. All ingredients are sold in Asian shops and larger supermarkets.

simple rolled sushi norimaki

8–inch piece unwaxed cucumber, or 2–3 kirby cucumbers, unpeeled

3 sheets nori seaweed

¾ recipe Vinegared Rice (page 11), divided into 3 portions

wasabi paste

HAND VINEGAR

¼ cup Japanese rice vinegar

1 cup water

TO SERVE

Pickled Ginger (page 123)

extra wasabi paste

Japanese soy sauce

a sushi rolling mat

MAKES 36 PIECES

1 Mix the hand vinegar ingredients in a small bowl and set aside.

2 To prepare the cucumber, cut into fourths lengthwise, then cut out the seeds and cut the remainder, lengthwise, into ½-inch square matchstick lengths. You need 6, each with some green skin.

3 Just before assembling, pass the nori over a very low gas flame or electric hotplate, just for a few seconds to make it crisp and bring out the flavor. Cut each sheet in half crosswise.

4 Assemble the rolls according to the method on the following pages.

5 Cut each roll into 6 pieces.

6 Arrange on a platter and serve with pickled ginger, a little pile of wasabi, and a dish of Japanese soy sauce.

making simple rolls step-by-step

Make the Vinegared Rice (page 11) and Hand Vinegar (page 13), then prepare and assemble the remaining ingredients.

1 Put a sushi rolling mat on a work surface, then put ½ sheet of toasted nori seaweed on top. Dip your fingers in the bowl of hand vinegar, then take a handful of the rice (2–3 heaping tablespoons) and make into a log shape. Put the rice in the middle of the nori.

2 Using your fingers, spread it evenly all over, leaving about ½-inch margin on the far side. (The rice will stick to your fingers, so dip them in the hand vinegar as necessary.)

3 Take a small dot of wasabi paste on the end of your finger and draw a line down the middle across the rice, leaving a light green shadow on top of the rice (not too much—wasabi is very hot!)

4 Arrange a strip of cucumber across the rice, on top of the wasabi.

5 Pick up the mat from the near side and keep the cucumber in the center.

6 Roll the mat over to meet the other side so that the rice stays inside the nori.

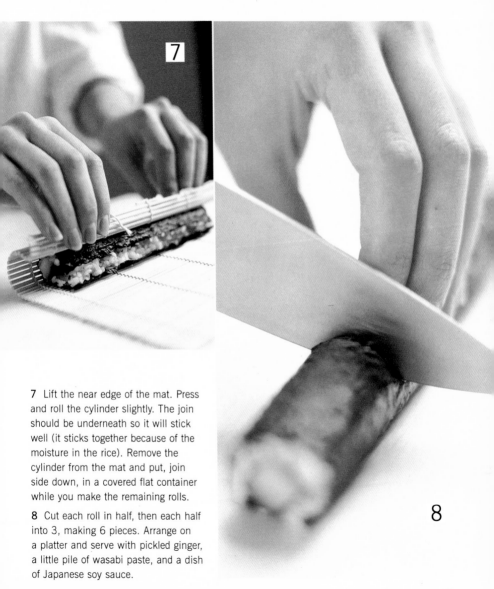

7 Lift the near edge of the mat. Press and roll the cylinder slightly. The join should be underneath so it will stick well (it sticks together because of the moisture in the rice). Remove the cylinder from the mat and put, join side down, in a covered flat container while you make the remaining rolls.

8 Cut each roll in half, then each half into 3, making 6 pieces. Arrange on a platter and serve with pickled ginger, a little pile of wasabi paste, and a dish of Japanese soy sauce.

Other ingredients traditionally used for rolled sushi in Japan include *kanpyo* (dried gourd ribbons), tuna with scallion, *natto* (steamed fermented soy beans), chile-marinated cod's roe, and *umeboshi* (salted plum) with shiso herb. You can also make variations using ingredients more readily available in the West.

rolled sushi variations

¾ recipe Vinegared Rice (page 11), divided into 3 portions

3 sheets nori seaweed

HAND VINEGAR

¼ cup Japanese rice vinegar

1 cup water

FILLINGS: YOUR CHOICE OF

4 oz. fresh salmon, skinned

2½ inches pickled daikon (takuan), cut lengthwise into ½-inch matchsticks

4–6 fresh shiso leaves or 6–8 basil leaves

2 small red pickled plums (umeboshi), pitted and torn in pieces

wasabi paste

TO SERVE

Pickled Ginger (page 123)

extra wasabi paste

Japanese soy sauce

a sushi rolling mat

MAKES 36 PIECES

1 Mix the hand vinegar ingredients in a small bowl and set aside.

2 Cut the piece of salmon into ½ inch square strips. To make a salmon sushi, follow the method on pages 16–17, using a row of salmon strips instead of cucumber. (Enough to make 2 rolls.)

3 To make a pickled daikon sushi, follow the method on pages 16–17, using 3 strips of pickled daikon in a row instead of cucumber, and omitting the wasabi paste. (Enough to make 2 rolls.)

4 To make the pickled plum sushi, follow the method on pages 16–17, using the shiso or basil leaves and the pieces of plum. (Enough to make 2 rolls.)

5 Cut each roll into 6 pieces, then arrange on a plate and serve with pickled ginger, a mound of wasabi, and a dish of soy sauce.

Note You can also leave the salmon fillet whole, then lightly broil it for about 2 minutes on each side. Cool, put in a bowl, flake with a fork, then stir in 2 finely chopped scallions. Mix in salt, pepper, and 2 teaspoons mayonnaise, then proceed as in the main recipe.

big sushi rolls futomaki

3 sheets nori seaweed

1 recipe Vinegared Rice
(page 11), divided into
6 portions

HAND VINEGAR

¼ cup Japanese rice vinegar

1 cup water

FILLINGS

9–12 uncooked jumbo
shrimp, unpeeled

1 recipe Japanese Omelet
(page 121)

8 oz. spinach,
about 2 cups leaves

3½ tablespoons Japanese
soy sauce

1 oz. dried gourd (kanpyo)
or 1 carrot, cut into
⅛-inch square shreds

5–6 dried shiitake mushrooms

2 tablespoons sugar

1 tablespoon mirin (Japanese
rice wine) or sweet sherry

sea salt

TO SERVE

Japanese soy sauce

Pickled Ginger (page 123)

toothpicks or bamboo skewers

a sushi rolling mat

MAKES 24 PIECES

1 Mix the hand vinegar ingredients in a small bowl and set aside.

2 Skewer a toothpick through each shrimp from head to tail to prevent curling while cooking. Blanch in boiling water for 3 minutes until firm and pink. Immediately plunge into cold water and drain. Remove and discard the toothpicks, shells, and dark back vein.

3 Cut the Japanese omelet lengthwise into ½-inch square sticks.

4 Blanch the spinach in lightly salted water for 1 minute. Plunge into cold water. Drain and pat dry with paper towels. Sprinkle with 2 teaspoons of the soy sauce and set aside.

5 If using dried gourd, rub it with salt and a little water, then soak in water for 10 minutes and drain. Cut into 8-inch lengths. Soak the shiitakes in warm water for 30 minutes, then drain, retaining the soaking water. Cut into 2-inch strips. Put 1 cup of the soaking liquid in a small saucepan with the remaining soy sauce, sugar, and mirin. Bring to a boil. Add the gourd and shiitakes. Simmer over low heat for 15 minutes. Let cool in the liquid.

6 Toast the nori over a low gas flame or hotplate and put it crosswise, on a sushi rolling mat, following the method on page 15. Dip your hands in the hand vinegar. Take 1 portion of the rice and squeeze it into a firm ball. Put the rice ball on one side of the nori sheet in the middle and, using wet fingers, spread evenly over the half side of nori, leaving 1 inch clear on the far side. Repeat once more to fill the other half. The rice should be fairly thick—add extra if necessary.

7 Arrange 3–4 shrimp in a row across the rice about 2 inches from the front edge. Add a row of omelet strips and a row of spinach on top of the shrimp. Add a row of gourd or carrot and a row of shiitakes on top, so that all 5 ingredients are piled in the center of the rice, like logs of wood. Each roll should use one-third of each ingredient.

8 Pick up the mat from the near side and roll the mat following the method on page 16. Remove the mat and put the roll on a plate, join side down. Repeat to make 2 more rolls. Cut each roll into 8 and serve with little dishes of soy sauce and pickled ginger.

children's favorites

Sushi is fun when you make it for or with children. Devising sushi for non-Japanese kids can lead to some surprise discoveries.

1 Mix the hand vinegar ingredients in a small bowl and set aside.

2 To make the fillings, strain the egg into a small bowl, add ½ tablespoon sugar and a pinch of salt, and beat until dissolved. Heat a skillet, brush with oil, and rub off any excess with paper towels.

3 Pour in the egg mixture and make a thin pancake, tilting the pan to spread it evenly. Prick any bubbles with a fork and fill any holes with egg by tilting the skillet. After 30 seconds, turn the omelet over for 30 seconds to dry the other side and make it golden yellow. Remove from the heat, remove with a spatula, and cut in half.

4 Blanch the carrot in about 1 cup boiling salted water for 2–3 minutes. Reduce the heat and stir in the remaining 1½ tablespoons sugar and a pinch of salt. Simmer for another 2–3 minutes, then remove from the heat and let cool in the juice.

5 Put half the omelet on a board with the cut side nearest you and put a row of carrot strips beside the cut edge. Roll up the omelet tightly and secure the end with a toothpick. Repeat to make a second roll.

6 Cook the hot dogs according to the package instructions and drain well on paper towels. Cut into ½-inch square matchsticks. Thickly peel the cucumber and finely shred the skin.

7 Put the canned salmon in a bowl, add the mayonnaise and pinch of salt, and stir well.

8 Following the method on page 15, make 2 sushi rolls with a carrot-and-egg-roll filling (remove the toothpicks first), 2 rolls with strips of hot dog, and 2 with salmon paste and cucumber.

9 Cut each roll into 6 pieces and serve with soy sauce.

3 sheets nori seaweed

¾ recipe Vinegared Rice (page 11), divided into 6 portions

3 sheets nori seaweed

Japanese soy sauce, to serve

HAND VINEGAR

¼ cup Japanese rice vinegar

1 cup water

FILLINGS

1 egg, beaten

2 tablespoons sugar

2½ inches carrot, sliced lengthwise into ⅛-inch matchsticks

2 thin hot dogs, 7 inches long, or 4 Vienna sausages, 4 inches long

2½ inches unwaxed cucumber or 1 kirby cucumber

3 oz. canned red salmon, drained

1 tablespoon mayonnaise

sea salt

safflower oil, for frying

a Japanese omelet pan or 8-inch nonstick skillet

a sushi rolling mat

MAKES 36 PIECES

This is a very Western idea of sushi, but it is easy and convenient because it uses canned tuna. Use real Japanese mayonnaise if you can, but homemade or good-quality mayonnaise from a jar works well.

wasabi mayonnaise and tuna roll

4 sheets nori seaweed

6 oz. canned albacore tuna in water, drained

4 teaspoons Japanese or other mayonnaise

1 teaspoon wasabi paste, or to taste

4 oz. baby corn, fresh or frozen, or equivalent drained canned baby corn

½ recipe Vinegared Rice (page 11), divided into 4 portions

HAND VINEGAR

¼ cup Japanese rice vinegar

1 cup water

a sushi rolling mat

MAKES 24–28 PIECES

1 Mix the hand vinegar ingredients in a small bowl and set aside.

2 Trim a 1-inch strip from one long edge of each sheet of nori and reserve for another use.

3 Put the tuna and mayonnaise in a bowl and stir in the wasabi.

4 If using fresh or frozen corn, bring a saucepan of water to a boil, and cook the corn for 3 minutes, or until tender. Drain and rinse under cold water to cool. If using canned corn, drain and rinse.

5 Put a sheet of nori, rough side up with the long edge towards you, on a sushi rolling mat. Dip your fingers in the hand vinegar, and top the nori with 1 portion of the vinegared rice, then spread it in a thin layer, leaving about ¾ inch of bare nori on the far edge. Spoon one-fourth of the tuna mixture in a line along the middle of the rice and top with a line of baby corn, set end to end.

6 Lift the edge of the mat closest to you and start rolling up the sushi away from you, pressing in the filling with your fingers as you roll. You may need a little water along the far edge to seal it. Repeat to make 4 rolls.

7 Using a clean, wet knife, slice each roll into 6–7 even pieces.

Fresh tuna is one of the most popular fillings for sushi. There are three main cuts of tuna, the pink *otoro* (the finest), *chutoro*, and the dark red *akami*. With their incredible popularity and high price tags, otoro and chutoro are delicacies reserved for sashimi, but the akami is perfect for rolled sushi.

spicy tuna roll

1 Mix the hand vinegar ingredients in a small bowl and set aside.

2 Slice the tuna into ½-inch strips and put in a shallow dish. Mix the soy sauce, sake, hot pepper sauce, and scallions in a bowl. Pour over the tuna and stir well to coat. Cover and let marinate for 30 minutes. Divide into 6 portions.

3 Put ½ sheet of nori, rough side up with the long edge towards you, on a sushi rolling mat. Dip your fingers in the hand vinegar, take 1 portion of the vinegared rice, and spread it in a thin layer over the nori, leaving about ¾ inch bare on the far edge. Set 1 portion of the tuna strips in a line along the middle of the rice.

4 Lift the edge of the mat closest to you and start rolling up the sushi away from you, pressing in the filling with your fingers as you roll. You may need a little water along the far edge to seal it. Repeat to make 6 rolls.

5 Using a clean, wet knife, slice each roll into 6–7 even pieces.

10 oz. fresh tuna

2 tablespoons Japanese soy sauce

1 tablespoon sake

1 teaspoon Chinese hot pepper sauce, or chile sauce

2 scallions, finely chopped

3 sheets nori seaweed, halved

½ recipe Vinegared Rice (page 11), divided into 6 portions

HAND VINEGAR

¼ cup Japanese rice vinegar

1 cup water

a sushi rolling mat

MAKES 36–42 PIECES

Soaking in vinegar is a way of mellowing the strong flavors of some fish, such as mackerel. If you don't have time to prepare fresh mackerel, try making this sushi with smoked mackerel or other smoked fish for a different, but still delicious flavor.

vinegared mackerel and avocado roll

1 lb. fresh mackerel fillets
(about 2 medium fillets)

2 tablespoons salt

⅓ cup Japanese rice vinegar

1 tablespoon sugar

1 avocado

3 sheets nori seaweed, halved

½ recipe Vinegared Rice
(page 11), divided into
6 portions

1 teaspoon wasabi paste
(optional)

HAND VINEGAR

¼ cup Japanese rice vinegar

1 cup water

a sushi rolling mat

MAKES 36–42 PIECES

1 Mix the hand vinegar ingredients in a small bowl and set aside.

2 Put the mackerel fillets in a shallow, non-metal bowl and sprinkle on both sides with the salt. Cover with plastic wrap and refrigerate for 8 hours or overnight.

3 Remove the fish from the refrigerator, rinse in cold running water, and pat dry with paper towels. Put the vinegar and sugar in a shallow dish, mix well, then add the mackerel, turning to coat. Let marinate for 40 minutes at room temperature.

4 Remove the fish from the marinade and slice diagonally into ½-inch strips. Slice the avocado into ½-inch strips.

5 Put a sheet of nori, rough side up with the long edge towards you, on a sushi rolling mat. Dip your fingers in the hand vinegar, take 1 portion of the vinegared rice and spread it out in a thin layer over the nori, leaving about ¾ inch bare on the far edge. Smear a little wasabi, if using, down the middle of the rice. Arrange a line of mackerel slices over the wasabi and top with a line of the avocado.

6 Lift the edge of the mat closest to you and start rolling the sushi away from you, pressing in the filling with your fingers as you roll. You may need a little water along the far edge to seal it. Repeat with the remaining ingredients to make 6 rolls. Using a clean, wet knife, slice each roll into 6–7 even pieces.

A fresh oyster makes such an elegantly simple topping for sushi. Choose small oysters if possible—large ones will swamp a delicate roll.

oyster roll
with chile cucumber

2 sheets nori seaweed

½ recipe Vinegared Rice (page 11), divided into 2 portions

freshly squeezed juice of 1 lemon

20 small raw oysters, shucked

CHILE CUCUMBER

½ cup Japanese white rice vinegar

2 tablespoons sugar

1 tablespoon mirin (sweetened Japanese rice wine)

3-inch piece cucumber, halved, seeded, and cut into fine matchsticks

2 small, mild red chiles, halved, seeded, and finely sliced

HAND VINEGAR

¼ cup Japanese rice vinegar

1 cup water

a sushi rolling mat

MAKES 20 PIECES

1 To make the chile cucumber, put the vinegar, sugar, and mirin in a small saucepan and bring to a boil, stirring. Reduce the heat and simmer for 3 minutes. Remove from the heat and let cool.

2 Put the cucumber and chiles in a plastic bowl and pour over the cooled vinegar mixture. Cover and refrigerate for 24 hours.

3 When ready to assemble the rolls, mix the hand vinegar ingredients in a small bowl and set aside.

4 Put a sheet of nori, rough side up with the long edge towards you, on a sushi rolling mat. Dip your fingers in the hand vinegar, take 1 portion of the vinegared rice and spread it out in a thin layer over the nori, leaving about ¾ inch bare on the far edge. Lift the edge of the mat closest to you and start rolling the sushi away from you. You may need a little water along the far edge to seal it. Press the roll into an oval. Repeat with the remaining ingredients to make a second roll.

5 Using a clean, wet knife, slice each roll in half, then each half into 5 even pieces, making 20 in all.

6 Sprinkle lemon juice over the oysters. Top each piece of sushi with an oyster and a little chile cucumber, then serve.

Uramaki is an "inside-out" roll, with nori inside and rice outside. This shrimp tempura version is popular in restaurants—the nori prevents the vinegar in the rice and the oil in the tempura from touching each other.

inside-out sushi uramaki

2 sheets nori seaweed

¾ recipe Vinegared Rice (page 11), divided into 4 poritions

HAND VINEGAR

2 tablespoons Japanese rice vinegar

½ cup water

TEMPURA SHRIMP

8 uncooked jumbo shrimp, 4 peeled completely, 4 left with tail fins intact, deveined

⅔ cup all-purpose flour, sifted

¼ cup sesame seeds, black or white

sea salt

safflower oil, for frying

TO SERVE

Pickled Ginger (page 123)

Japanese soy sauce

8 toothpicks or bamboo skewers

a sushi rolling mat covered with plastic wrap

MAKES 20 PIECES

1 Mix the hand vinegar ingredients in a small bowl. Skewer a toothpick through each shrimp from top to tail to prevent curling while cooking.

2 Cover one side of a sushi rolling mat with plastic wrap and put it on a dry cutting board, plastic side up.

3 Fill a wok or deep saucepan one-third full of oil and heat to 340°F or until a cube of bread browns in about 60 seconds. To make the tempura batter, put ½ cup water in a bowl, sift the flour into the water, and mix with a fork. One by one, dip the shrimp in the batter, then fry in the hot oil for 3–4 minutes or until golden brown. Remove and drain on paper towels and carefully remove and discard the toothpicks.

4 Put the nori on a completely dry cutting board. Take a handful of the rice (2–3 heaping tablespoons) and make into a log shape. Dip your fingers in the hand vinegar. Put the rice in the center of the nori. Using your fingers, spread it evenly all over, right to the edges. Sprinkle 1 tablespoon sesame seeds all over the rice.

5 Turn the whole thing over onto the plastic-covered mat.

6 Arrange 2 tempura shrimp down the center of the nori, with the tails sticking out at the ends (remove the tail fins if you like).

7 Roll the mat following the method on page 16–17. Remove from the mat and repeat to make 3 more rolls.

8 Cut each roll into 5 pieces and arrange on a platter. Serve with pickled ginger and a little soy sauce in a small dish beside the platter or in small individual plates.

slow-cooked squid

Squid is delicious in sushi, but can be tricky when raw, because it does tend to be tough. If you braise it slowly, you end up with deliciously tender pieces.

8 oz. baby squid tubes, 3 inches long (about 12), cleaned

1 teaspoon mirin (sweetened Japanese rice wine)

1 teaspoon soy sauce

½ teaspoon finely chopped fresh red chile

½ teaspoon finely chopped garlic

1 teaspoon grated fresh ginger

1 tablespoon finely chopped cilantro

½ recipe Vinegared Rice (page 11)

1 tablespoon black sesame seeds

HAND VINEGAR

¼ cup Japanese rice vinegar

1 cup water

baking sheet with sides or broiler pan

MAKES 24 PIECES

1 Slice the squid bodies in half lengthwise and arrange on a baking sheet or broiler pan. Sprinkle with the mirin and soy. Set the tray at least 6 inches away from a preheated broiler so the heat is not too fierce. Broil for about 8 minutes or until the squid turns opaque. Remove and let cool.

2 Put the squid in a bowl, add the chile, garlic, ginger, and cilantro, stir gently, cover, and let marinate in the refrigerator for 1 hour.

3 Mix the hand vinegar ingredients in a small bowl and set aside.

4 Dip your fingers in the hand vinegar and divide the rice into 24 walnut-size balls.

5 Top each rice ball with a piece of squid using the natural curl of the squid body to hold it securely. Sprinkle each with a few black sesame seeds, then serve.

Yakitori is the name given to food broiled on skewers over a charcoal fire. It can be anything—chicken, steak, liver, or the octopus used here. Shrimp, scallops, or any firm fish also work well.

yakitori octopus roll

6 octopus tentacles, about 2 lb, tenderized, skin and suckers removed

6 scallions

2 tablespoons sake

2 tablespoons Japanese soy sauce

1 teaspoon sugar

1 teaspoon freshly grated ginger

3 sheets nori seaweed, halved

½ recipe Vinegared Rice (page 11), divided into 6 portions

HAND VINEGAR

¼ cup Japanese rice vinegar

1 cup water

5 bamboo skewers, soaked in water for 30 minutes

a sushi rolling mat

MAKES 30 PIECES

1 Cut the octopus into 1-inch pieces. Cut the scallions into 1 inch lengths. Thread the pieces of octopus and scallion crosswise alternately onto the soaked skewers.

2 Put the sake, soy, sugar and ginger in a small bowl or pitcher, mix well, then pour over the octopus skewers and let marinate at room temperature for 30 minutes, turning occasionally.

3 Preheat an outdoor grill or the broiler to very hot. Set the yakitori skewers about 3 inches from the heat and cook for 4–5 minutes, turning once. Remove from the heat and let cool.

4 Mix the hand vinegar ingredients in a small bowl and set aside.

5 Put a sheet of nori, rough side up with the long edge towards you, on a sushi rolling mat. Dip your fingers in the hand vinegar and add 1 portion of the vinegared rice, spread in a thin layer over the nori, leaving about ¾ inch bare on the far edge. Arrange pieces of octopus, end to end, in a line along the middle of the rice, then put a line of scallions on top.

6 Lift the edge of the mat closest to you and start rolling up the sushi away from you, pressing in the filling with your fingers as you roll. You may need a little water along the far edge to seal it. Repeat to make 6 rolls. Using a clean, wet knife, slice each roll into 5 even pieces.

Note If the octopus has not been pre-tenderized, you can either beat it with a meat mallet or try this Portuguese method. Wash well and put in a large saucepan with 1 sliced onion. Cover with a lid and slowly bring to a boil over low heat (there will be enough moisture in the octopus to do this without added water). Let simmer for 30–40 minutes until the tender. Cool, then pull off and discard the purple skin and suckers.

To many sushi fans, delicious raw fish is part of the pleasure of this dish. However, if you're not an aficionado of fish *au naturel*, using smoked or pickled fish is a delicious compromise. It is very easy to pickle fish at home, and you can control the sharpness more easily.

pickled salmon roll

1 To prepare the salmon, put the vinegar, salt, sugar, and lemon zest in a saucepan with ¼ cup water. Bring to a boil, reduce the heat, then simmer for 3 minutes. Let cool.

2 Put the salmon fillet in a plastic container with the shallots. Pour the vinegar mixture over the top and cover tightly. Refrigerate for 2–3 days, turning the salmon in the pickle once a day.

3 When ready to make the sushi, drain the salmon and shallots. Slice the salmon as finely as possible and divide into 6 portions.

4 Mix the hand vinegar ingredients in a small bowl and set aside.

5 Put ½ sheet of nori, rough side up with the long edge towards you, on a sushi rolling mat. Dip your fingers in the hand vinegar, then take 1 portion of the vinegared rice and spread it out in a thin layer over the nori, leaving about ¾ inch bare at the far edge. Smear a little wasabi down the center of the rice if you like. Arrange 1 portion of the salmon slices in a line along the middle of the rice and top with a line of the pickled shallots.

6 Lift the edge of the mat closest to you and start rolling the sushi away from you, pressing in the filling with your fingers as you roll. You may need a little water along the far edge to seal it. Repeat with the remaining ingredients to make 6 rolls.

7 Using a clean wet knife, slice each roll into 6–7 even pieces, then serve.

3 sheets nori seaweed, halved

½ recipe Vinegared Rice (page 11), divided into 6 portions

1 teaspoon wasabi paste (optional)

PICKLED SALMON

½ cup Japanese white rice vinegar

2 teaspoons sea salt

2 tablespoons sugar

zest of 1 unwaxed lemon, removed with a lemon zester

10 oz. salmon fillet, skinned and boned

4 shallots, finely sliced

HAND VINEGAR

¼ cup Japanese rice vinegar

1 cup water

a sushi rolling mat

MAKES 36–42 PIECES

tempura shrimp roll

The crunch of tempura batter is delicious in sushi, although the batter will soften as it cools. If you have some leftover batter, use it to cook vegetables or for the tempura croutons for miso soup on page 117.

24 large uncooked shrimp, peeled, but with tail fins intact

2 sheets nori seaweed

½ recipe Vinegared Rice (page 11)

1 teaspoon wasabi (optional)

1 cup mizuna or baby spinach

peanut or safflower oil, for frying

TEMPURA BATTER

1 egg, separated

1 tablespoon lemon juice

⅔ cup ice water

scant ⅓ cup all-purpose flour

HAND VINEGAR

¼ cup Japanese rice vinegar

1 cup water

24 bamboo skewers

MAKES 24 PIECES

1 Fill a large wok or saucepan one-third full of oil and heat to 375°F, or until a small cube of bread turns golden in 30 seconds.

2 Thread each shrimp onto a skewer to straighten it for cooking.

3 To make the batter, put the egg yolk, lemon juice, and ice water in a bowl. Whisk gently, then whisk in the flour to form a smooth batter. Do not overmix.

4 Whisk the egg white in a second bowl until stiff but not dry, then fold into the batter.

5 Dip each shrimp in the batter and fry for 1–2 minutes until crisp and golden. Drain on crumpled paper towels and let cool for 5 minutes. Remove the skewers.

6 Mix the hand vinegar ingredients in a small bowl and set aside.

7 Using dry hands, cut the nori sheets in half crosswise and then into 1-inch strips. Dip your fingers in the hand vinegar and spread about 1 tablespoon of rice over each piece of nori, top with a tempura shrimp, a dab of wasabi, if using, and a little mizuna or baby spinach. Roll up to secure the filling. Brush the nori with water to help it stick, if necessary. Repeat until all the ingredients have been used.

This battleship-shaped version of nigiri-zushi (page 49) has a ribbon of nori seaweed wrapped vertically around the rice and raw toppings such as salmon caviar (*ikura* or *keta*) and sea urchin. This recipe includes Western variations using crab lumpmeat and flaked crabmeat.

battleship rolls
gunkanmaki

1½ sheets nori seaweed

½ recipe Vinegared Rice (page 11)

HAND VINEGAR

¼ cup Japanese rice vinegar

1 cup water

TOPPINGS

½–⅔ cup crabmeat*

about 1 teaspoon sake

2 teaspoons wasabi paste

¼–⅓ cup salmon caviar (ikura or keta) or red lumpfish caviar

12 pickled caper berries or capers

TO SERVE

Pickled Ginger (page 123)

Japanese soy sauce

MAKES 12 PIECES

*Use the "fresh" lump crabmeat sold in a tub in fish stores, not the pasteurized canned variety.

1 Mix the hand vinegar ingredients in a small bowl and set aside.

2 Put the crabmeat on a small plates and sprinkle with a little sake. If using wasabi powder, mix 1–2 teaspoons powder in an egg cup with about 1–2 teaspoons water to make a clay-like consistency. Turn it upside down and set aside to prevent it drying out.

3 Cut each sheet of nori crosswise into ribbons, 7 x 1 inches, making 12 ribbons in total.

4 Dip your hands in the hand vinegar and take 1–2 tablespoons of the cooked rice in one hand. Mold it into a rectangular mound about 2 x ¾ x 1¼ inches high. Wrap a nori ribbon around it, overlapping about ¾ inch at the end. Glue it together with a grain of vinegared rice. Put 2 teaspoons caviar and a few pickled caper berries or capers on top. Repeat to make 3 more rolls with caviar, 4 with crabmeat topped with a little salmon caviar, and 4 with crabmeat with a dot of wasabi on top.

5 Arrange on a platter, and serve with the pickled ginger and a small dish of soy sauce as party food. If making individual servings, serve the soy sauce in small, separate dishes.

Battleship sushi is individually hand rolled, so the nori comes about a quarter-inch above the rice, leaving room for less manageable toppings such as caviar. Small cubes of differently colored fish make a pretty topping and you don't need to be an expert fish slicer to get tender pieces. You do, however, need very fresh raw fish—that is what "sushi- or sashimi-grade" means. If you have access to a real Japanese fish seller, that's perfect. Otherwise, go to a fish market, or other outlet, where you can be sure the fish is ultra-fresh.

3 oz. piece of sashimi-grade raw salmon

3 oz. piece of sashimi-grade raw tuna

3 oz. piece of sashimi-grade raw white fish (try sea bass, turbot, or halibut)

½ recipe Vinegared Rice (page 11)

4 sheets nori seaweed

1 teaspoon wasabi paste (optional)

1 tablespoon salmon caviar (ikura or keta)

HAND VINEGAR

¼ cup Japanese rice vinegar

1 cup water

MAKES 18 PIECES

treasures of the sea battleship sushi

1 Cut the salmon, tuna, and white fish into ¼-inch cubes, put them in a bowl, and mix gently.

2 Mix the hand vinegar ingredients in a small bowl.

3 Dip your fingers in the hand vinegar and divide the vinegared rice into 18 portions, a little smaller than a table tennis ball. Gently squeeze each piece into a flattened oval shape, about 1 inch high. With dry hands, cut the nori sheets into 1-inch strips, and wrap each piece of rice in one strip with the rough side of the nori facing inwards. Seal the ends with a dab of water. You should have about ¼ inch of nori above the rice.

4 Put a dab of wasabi, if using, on top of the rice, then add a heaping teaspoon of the fish cubes and a little salmon caviar.

Battleship rolls can be made with lettuce leaves instead of nori. Use iceberg to make cups and a lettuce with flexible leaves, such as Boston lettuce or leaf lettuce, to make ribbons.

lettuce rolls

1 Mix the hand vinegar ingredients in a small bowl and set aside.

2 Put the smoked trout or haddock and bay leaf in a saucepan, cover with boiling water, return to a boil, then simmer for 5 minutes or until cooked. Drain well. Remove and discard the skin and all the small bones. Put in a bowl and flake finely with a fork. Stir in the sugar and let cool.

3 Sprinkle the smoked salmon with lemon juice.

4 Cut a 1-inch-wide strip crosswise from the top of the frilly leaves and Boston lettuce leaves. Make a small cup, 3 inches in diameter, from the inner iceberg leaves.

5 Dip your fingers in the hand vinegar and make 12 rectangular mounds of rice, following the method on page 43. Instead of wrapping in nori, wrap 4 in frilly lettuce leaves, 4 in Boston lettuce leaves, and 4 in iceberg lettuce cups. Put 1–1½ tablespoons of fish flakes on top of the rice in the frilly lettuce. Put about 1–1½ tablespoons smoked salmon on the rice in the Boston lettuce, and about 1–1½ tablespoons caviar in the iceberg cups. Top the smoked fish with a little caviar, the salmon with a caper berry or caper, and the caviar with a few flakes of smoked fish.

6 Arrange on a platter or small plates and serve with a small dish of soy sauce.

½ recipe Vinegared Rice (page 11)

4 frilly lettuce leaves, such as oak leaf

4 Boston lettuce leaves

4 small iceberg lettuce leaves

Japanese soy sauce, to serve

HAND VINEGAR

¼ cup Japanese rice vinegar

1 cup water

TOPPINGS

3 oz. smoked fish, such as trout or haddock

1 bay leaf

1 teaspoon sugar

3 oz. smoked salmon, finely chopped

1 tablespoon lemon juice

¼–⅓ cup black lumpfish caviar

1 tablespoon caper berries or capers, drained

MAKES 12 PIECES

hand-molded sushi nigiri

Nigiri is the king of all sushi. Though it looks simple, it is actually the most difficult to make and is not usually made at home, even in Japan.

1 Mix the hand vinegar ingredients in a small bowl and set aside.

2 Push a bamboo skewer through each shrimp from top to tail to prevent curling while cooking. Blanch in boiling water for 2 minutes until lightly cooked and pink. Drain and put under running water. Remove and discard the toothpicks, shells, and back vein. Make a slit up the belly lengthwise and open out.

3 Slice the tuna or salmon and sea bream into rectangular pieces, 3 x 1 x ½ inch thick. Cut the squid into similar rectangular pieces and make fine slits on one side of each piece to make the squid more tender.

4 Using the beaten eggs, dashi, mirin, and soy sauce, make an omelet following the method on page 121. Put the rolled omelet on a sushi rolling mat and tightly roll into a flat rectangular shape. When cool, cut 2 rectangular pieces, 3 x 1 x ½ inch thick.

5 If using wasabi powder, mix with 2 teaspoons water in an egg cup and stir well to make a clay-like consistency. Leave upside down to prevent drying.

6 Dip your hands in the hand vinegar and take 1–2 tablespoons of the cooked rice in one hand and mold it into a rectangular cylinder about 2 x 1 x 1 inch. Put a tiny bit of wasabi on top and cover with an opened shrimp.

7 Repeat, making 2 nigiri topped with shrimp, 2 with tuna or salmon, 2 with sea bream, 2 with squid on top of a shiso leaf, and 2 with omelet. When assembling the nigiri with omelet, do not add wasabi: instead, tie with a thin nori ribbon, about ⅛ inch wide.

8 Arrange on a platter and serve with pickled ginger and Japanese soy sauce in a small dish. Alternatively, serve as party canapés or on small plates as part of a meal.

½ recipe Vinegared Rice (page 11)

HAND VINEGAR

¼ cup Japanese rice vinegar

1 cup water

JAPANESE OMELET

2 eggs, beaten

2 tablespoons Dashi (page 109)

1 teaspoon mirin (sweetened Japanese rice wine) or sweet sherry

1 teaspoon Japanese soy sauce

TOPPINGS

2 uncooked medium shrimp

1 fillet fresh tuna or salmon, about 4 oz., skinned

1 fillet fresh white-fleshed fish, such as fluke, flounder, or sole, about 4 oz., skinned

4 oz. squid, cleaned and skinned

2 teaspoons wasabi paste

2 shiso leaves or basil leaves

a small piece of nori seaweed, cut into ⅛-inch strips

sea salt

TO SERVE

Pickled Ginger (page 123)

Japanese soy sauce

2 bamboo skewers

a sushi rolling mat

MAKES 8–10 PIECES

lettuce boats

½ recipe Vinegared Rice
(page 11)

HAND VINEGAR

¼ cup Japanese rice vinegar

1 cup water

TOPPINGS

4 oz. tender beef, such as
filet mignon, about
3 inches thick

vegetable oil, for rubbing

ice water

1–2 rollmops (marinated
Bismarck herring)

8 asparagus tips

2 teaspoons wasabi paste

4 mini romaine lettuce leaves

8 small Belgian endive leaves

TO SERVE

sprigs of watercress or
shredded scallions

a small strip of nori seaweed

1 scallion, finely chopped

1 inch fresh ginger,
peeled and grated

2 tablespoons white wine

1½ tablespoons Japanese
soy sauce

freshly squeezed juice
of ½ lemon

MAKES 12 PIECES

1 Mix the hand vinegar ingredients in a small bowl and set aside.

2 Rub the beef all over with vegetable oil. Broil or cook in a stove-top grill pan at a high heat until golden brown on all sides, but rare in the middle. Plunge into ice water to stop the cooking. Remove from the water, pat dry with paper towels, and cut 4 thin slices, about 3 x 2 inches. All the slices should be red inside and brown around the edges.

3 Cut the rollmops into 4 and make a little lengthwise slit in the skin of each piece.

4 Cook the asparagus in lightly salted water for 5 minutes until soft. Drain and put under running water to arrest cooking and bring out the color. Pat dry with paper towels.

5 If using wasabi powder, mix with 2 teaspoons water in an egg cup, stir to make a clay-like consistency, then turn upside down to stop it drying out.

6 Dip your hands in the hand vinegar and take a handful of the cooked rice in one hand (1–2 tablespoons). Mold it into a rectangle about 2 x 1 x 1 inch. Repeat with the remaining rice, making 12 portions. Put a tiny dab of wasabi on top of 4 portions.

7 Arrange a slice of beef on 1 portion of wasabi and rice, with the 2 short sides hanging over the end. Top with a few sprigs of cress. Repeat with the other 3 slices of beef and set them in 4 mini romaine lettuce leaves.

8 Arrange 2 asparagus tips on another rice portion and tie with a nori ribbon. Repeat to make 3 more. Arrange a piece of rollmop on each of the remaining 4 rice portions and insert chopped scallion and grated ginger into the slits. Arrange all the leaf boats on a serving platter. To make a lemon sauce, mix the white wine, soy sauce, and the lemon juice in a small bowl. Serve the lettuce boats with a small bowl of lemon sauce and another of plain soy sauce.

teriyaki chicken roll
with miso dipping sauce

1 To make the teriyaki sauce, mix the soy, mirin and chicken broth in a small saucepan and bring to a boil. Remove from the heat and let cool.

2 To make the teriyaki glaze, mix the sugar and cornstarch in a small bowl with a little cold water, then stir in 2 tablespoons of the teriyaki sauce. Set aside.

3 Thread the strips of chicken onto the soaked skewers, then brush with half the teriyaki sauce and marinate for 10 minutes. Preheat a broiler or outdoor grill to very hot. Set the chicken skewers under or over the heat. Cook for 2–3 minutes, turn the skewers over, and brush with more sauce and cook for a further 2–3 minutes until cooked. Remove from the heat, pour over the teriyaki glaze, let cool, then unthread. The chicken must be cold.

4 Mix the hand vinegar ingredients in a small bowl and set aside.

5 Set a sheet of nori, rough side up with the long edge towards you, on a sushi rolling mat. Dip your fingers in the hand vinegar, take 1 portion of the vinegared rice and spread in a thin layer covering about half of the nori closest to you. Put one-quarter of the chicken in a line along the middle of the rice and smear with a little wasabi.

6 Lift the edge of the mat closest to you and start rolling up the sushi away from you, pressing in the filling with your fingers as you roll. You may need a little water along the far edge to seal it. Repeat with the remaining ingredients, to make 4 rolls. Using a clean wet knife, slice each roll into 6–7 even pieces.

7 To make the white miso dipping sauce, put the miso, sugar, and sake in a small saucepan over medium heat. Bring to a simmer, reduce the heat to low, and cook for 3 minutes, stirring constantly to stop it burning. Remove from the heat, quickly stir in the egg yolk, strain if necessary, and let cool before serving with the sushi.

14 oz. boneless, skinless chicken thigh or breast (2 breasts, 4 thighs), cut into ½-inch strips

4 sheets nori seaweed

½ recipe Vinegared Rice (page 11) divided into 4 portions

1 teaspoon wasabi paste

TERIYAKI SAUCE

2 tablespoons Japanese soy sauce

2 tablespoons mirin (sweetened Japanese rice wine)

2 tablespoons chicken broth

TERIYAKI GLAZE

1 teaspoon sugar

½ teaspoon cornstarch

miso dipping sauce

2 tablespoons white miso paste

1 tablespoon sugar

½ cup sake

1 small egg yolk

HAND VINEGAR

¼ cup Japanese rice vinegar

1 cup water

12 bamboo skewers soaked in water for 30 minutes

a sushi rolling mat

MAKES 24–28 PIECES

Pickled plums (*umeboshi*) can be bought in health food stores and Japanese and Asian supermarkets. They can be very salty and sharp, so you don't need too much. If you do not like the flavor of pickled plum, replace with pickled ginger.

sushi balls with roast pork and pickled plums

2 tablespoons Japanese soy sauce

1 tablespoon mirin (sweetened Japanese rice wine)

1 teaspoon Chinese hot pepper sauce or chile sauce

8 oz. pork tenderloin, in one piece

½ recipe Vinegared Rice (page 11)

10 Japanese pickled plums, halved and pitted

HAND VINEGAR

¼ cup Japanese rice vinegar

1 cup water

a roasting pan

MAKES 20 PIECES

1 Put the pork in a plastic container. Mix the soy, mirin, and hot pepper sauce in a bowl or pitcher, then pour over the pork. Set aside to marinate for 1 hour, turning the pork in the marinade every 15 minutes.

2 Put the pork in a roasting pan and pour the marinade over the top. Roast in a preheated oven to 400°F for 15 minutes. Remove from the oven, let cool, then slice thinly—you should get about 20 slices.

3 Mix the hand vinegar ingredients in a small bowl and set aside.

4 Dip your fingers in the hand vinegar and divide the rice into 20 balls. Take a piece of pickled plum and push it into the center of a rice ball, then mold the rice around it so it is completely hidden. Repeat with the remaining plums and rice. Top each ball with a slice of roast pork, then serve.

marinated beef sushi (beef tataki)

Beef tataki is very rare marinated beef served in the sashimi style. If you do not like very rare beef, cook the fillet in a preheated oven at 350 °F for 10 minutes before returning to the pan to coat with sauce.

2 teaspoons peanut oil

10 oz. beef tenderloin, in one piece

2 tablespoons Japanese soy sauce

2 tablespoons mirin (sweetened Japanese rice wine)

2 tablespoons Japanese rice vinegar

½ recipe Vinegared Rice (page 11)

shredded Pickled Ginger (page 123), to serve (optional)

PICKLED RED CABBAGE

about ⅛ red cabbage

½ cup brown sugar

½ cup red wine vinegar

HAND VINEGAR

¼ cup Japanese rice vinegar

1 cup water

MAKES 18 SUSHI PIECES, 1 CUP PICKLED CABBAGE

1 To make the pickled red cabbage, finely slice the cabbage, removing any large core pieces, and chop into 1-inch lengths. Put in a medium saucepan, then add the brown sugar, vinegar, and ¼ cup water. Bring to a boil, reduce the heat, and simmer for 30 minutes.

2 Remove from the heat, let cool, and store in a sealed container in the refrigerator for up to 1 week, or in the freezer for 3 months.

3 To prepare the beef, heat the oil in a skillet and sear the beef on all sides until browned. Mix the soy sauce, mirin, and vinegar in a bowl and pour over the beef, turning the beef to coat. Remove immediately from the heat and transfer the beef and its sauce to a dish. Let cool, cover, and refrigerate for 1 hour, turning once.

4 Mix the hand vinegar ingredients in a small bowl and set aside.

5 Dip your fingers in the hand vinegar and divide the rice into 18 walnut-size balls, and shape into firm ovals.

6 Cut the beef in half lengthwise (along the natural separation line), then slice as finely as possible. Wrap a piece of beef around the top of a rice ball and top with a little pickled cabbage or ginger.

A perfect sushi for parties. Serve the rice, nori sheets, and prepared ingredients on plates and let people roll their own. Choose ingredients with varied tastes and colors. This is a delicious variation of the hand roll—using smoked salmon instead of crabsticks.

smoked salmon hand rolls temaki

¾ recipe Vinegared Rice (page 11)

4 sheets nori seaweed or 8 salad leaves

Pickled Ginger (page 123), to serve

HAND ROLL FILLINGS

4 oz. smoked salmon

4 scallions

2½ inches pickled daikon (takuan) or cucumber

1 avocado

freshly squeezed juice of 1 lemon

MAKES 8 ROLLS

1 Cut the smoked salmon lengthwise into ⅛-inch strips.

2 Finely slice the scallions lengthwise into 3–4-inch strips. Slice the pickled daikon or cucumber thinly.

3 Cut the avocado in half, remove the pit, and peel carefully. Thinly slice the flesh and brush with lemon juice.

4 Toast the nori sheets by quickly passing over a low flame to make them crisp and bring out the flavor. Cut each sheet in half crosswise.

5 Put the rice in a serving bowl and arrange salmon, scallion, and avocado on a serving platter. Put the nori and pickled ginger on small separate plates.

6 To assemble, follow the step-by-step directions on the following pages.

assembling hand rolls step-by-step

1 Take one piece of nori seaweed in one hand and add 2–3 tablespoons of vinegared rice. Spread the rice over half the nori.

2 Arrange your choice of fillings diagonally over the rice from the center to the outer corner.

3 Take the bottom right-hand corner and curl it towards the middle to form a cone.

4 Keep rolling the cone until complete. To glue the cone closed (optional), put a few grains of rice on the edge of the nori, and press together.

5 When the cone is complete, add your choice of a few drops of soy sauce, a few pieces of pickled ginger, and a dab of wasabi paste.

california roll

Oboro are fine white fish flakes, usually colored pink, making them perfect for adding a splash of color to sushi. These tiny hand rolls are very easy to eat with your fingers, and so make perfect party food. If you mix all the ingredients before rolling the sushi, the process will be a lot easier.

3-inch piece of cucumber

6 oz. crabmeat, fresh or canned

1 small or ½ medium (firm) avocado, cut into small cubes

½ recipe Vinegared Rice (page 11)

6–7 sheets nori seaweed

1 teaspoon wasabi paste (optional)

1 tablespoon oboro (optional, see recipe introduction)

MAKES 60–70 ROLLS

1 Slice the cucumber in half lengthwise and scrape out the seeds. Chop the flesh into tiny cubes and put in a bowl. Add the crabmeat, avocado, and rice and mix gently.

2 Cut each sheet of nori in half lengthwise, then cut the halves into 5 pieces crosswise (4 x 1½ inches).

3 Put 1 piece of nori, rough side up with the long edge towards you, on a work surface.

4 Spread 1 teaspoon of the rice mixture crosswise over the nori about one-quarter of the way in from the left edge. Smear the rice with a little wasabi, if using.

5 Take the bottom left corner of the nori and fold it diagonally so the left edge meets the top edge, then continue folding the whole triangle.

6 Sprinkle the open end with a little oboro, if using. Repeat until all the ingredients have been used.

This larger hand roll is still small enough to be held and eaten easily, but also makes a great appetizer or lunch if you allow 3 rolls per person. Choose any smoked fish, but make sure it is moist and soft.

smoked fish hand roll

1 Put the onion in a small saucepan with the vinegar and ¼ cup water. Bring to a boil, drain, and let cool.

2 Cut the smoked fish into strips, about 2 x ½ inch—you should have about 18 even pieces.

3 Quarter the cucumber lengthwise, scrape out the seeds, then cut into fine strips using a mandoline or vegetable peeler.

4 Cut each sheet of nori into 3 pieces (3 x 7 inches).

5 Put a piece of nori, rough side up with the long edge towards you, on a work surface. Spread 1 small, heaping teaspoon of rice crosswise over the nori about one-quarter of the way in from the left edge. Smear with a little wasabi, if using. Top the rice with a piece of fish, a few strips of carrot, red pepper and cucumber and a little red onion, pressing slightly into the rice to hold it firm while you roll.

6 Take the bottom left corner of the nori and fold it diagonally so the left edge meets the top edge, continue folding the whole triangle. Arrange with the join downwards on a serving plate or tray. Repeat to make 18 rolls altogether.

7 Serve with soy sauce.

1 small red onion, finely sliced

1 tablespoon rice vinegar

7 oz. smoked fish,
such as trout, salmon, or eel

2-inch piece of cucumber

6 sheets nori seaweed,
about 8 x 7 inches

½ recipe Vinegared Rice
(page 11)

1 teaspoon wasabi paste
(optional)

1 small carrot, finely sliced
into thin strips

1 small red bell pepper,
finely sliced into thin strips

MAKES 18 ROLLS

Sushi cones are a stylish way to serve sushi for a party, and the best way to use tiny Japanese mushrooms like hon-shigiri and enoki. Their delicate clusters of nodding heads would be completely lost in a rolled sushi.

sushi cones

4 sheets nori seaweed, halved (4 x 7 inches) and toasted

½ recipe Vinegared Rice (page 11)

Japanese soy sauce, to serve

HAND VINEGAR

¼ cup Japanese rice vinegar

1 cup water

FILLINGS SUCH AS

enoki mushrooms, raw or smoked salmon, blanched asparagus, finely sliced carrot, cucumber strips, thin Japanese Omelet (page 121), sliced, sesame seeds, wasabi, and Pickled Ginger (page 123)

MAKES 8 CONES

1 Mix the hand vinegar ingredients in a small bowl and set aside.

2 Put a sheet of nori, rough side up, on a work surface. Put 1 tablespoon rice on the left edge. Dip your fingers in the hand vinegar, then spread the rice lightly to cover half of the seaweed completely. Add your choice of filling ingredients diagonally across the rice, letting them overlap the top left corner.

3 To roll the cones, put one finger in the middle of the bottom edge, then roll up the cone from the bottom left, using your finger as the axis of the turn. As each cone is made, wet the outer edge with a finger dipped in hand vinegar, add a dot of rice to help seal it, then roll shut. Put it on a serving platter with the join side down.

4 Serve with soy sauce for dipping.

VEGETARIAN ROLLS

Futo-maki (thick rolled) sushi are great for lunch, because they are more substantial than *hosi-maki* (thin rolled).

five-color roll

½ oz. dried gourd (kampyo)

2 teaspoons salt, for rubbing

1 cup dashi or fish stock

2 teaspoons Japanese soy sauce

2 teaspoons mirin (sweetened Japanese rice wine)

1 teaspoon sugar

3 large eggs

a pinch of salt

2 teaspoons peanut oil

1½ cups spinach leaves, washed

3 sheets nori seaweed

½ recipe Vinegared Rice (page 11), divided into 3 portions

1 small red bell pepper, halved, seeded, and cut into fine strips

1 medium carrot, grated or very thinly sliced

HAND VINEGAR

¼ cup Japanese rice vinegar

1 cup water

a 20-inch skillet with a lid

MAKES 24 PIECES

1 Mix the hand vinegar ingredients in a small bowl and set aside.

2 Fill a bowl with water, add the gourd, rub the salt into the gourd to wash it, then drain and rinse thoroughly. Cover the gourd with fresh water and soak for 1 hour. Drain, then put in a saucepan, cover with boiling water, and cook for 5 minutes. Drain, return to the pan, then add the dashi, 1 teaspoon of the soy, 1 teaspoon of the mirin, and the sugar. Bring to a boil, reduce the heat, and simmer for 5 minutes. Let cool in the liquid, then drain.

3 Put the eggs in a bowl, add the salt and remaining soy and mirin, and mix well. Heat the oil in the pan or skillet over medium heat. Pour in the eggs, swirling the pan so the mixture covers the base. Cook for 2–3 minutes, gently gathering in the cooked omelet around the edges to let the uncooked egg run onto the hot pan. When the egg is set, take off the heat and fold in the 4 sides, so they meet in the middle and the omelet is now double thickness and square. Remove to a board, let cool, then slice into 3 strips.

4 Wipe out and reheat the pan. Add the washed but still wet spinach and cover with a lid. Cook for 1½–2 minutes until wilted. Tip into a colander and let cool for a few minutes. Using your hands, squeeze out the liquid from the spinach.

5 Put 1 sheet of nori, rough side up with the long edge towards you, on a sushi rolling mat. Dip your fingers in the hand vinegar, take 1 portion of the vinegared rice and spread it out in a thin layer over the nori, leaving 1 inch of nori bare at the far edge. Put a strip of omelet in the middle and put one-third of the gourd, spinach, pepper, and carrot, laid in lengthwise strips on top.

6 Pick up the mat from the near side and roll it following the method on pages 16–17. Wet the bare edge of nori and finish rolling to seal. Remove the mat and put the rool on a plate, join side down. Repeat to make 3 rolls and cut each one into 8 pieces.

cucumber sushi

This simple, traditional sushi is a favorite with vegetarians.

1 sheet nori seaweed, toasted

1 recipe Vinegared Rice (page 11), divided into 2 portions

½ teaspoon wasabi paste

1 mini cucumber, seeded and sliced lengthwise

HAND VINEGAR

¼ cup Japanese rice vinegar

1 cup water

TO SERVE

Japanese soy sauce

Pickled Ginger (page 123)

wasabi paste

a sushi rolling mat

MAKES 12 PIECES

1 Mix the hand vinegar ingredients in a small bowl and set aside.

2 Toast the nori over a gas flame or hotplate and cut it in half. Put one piece on a sushi rolling mat.

3 Dip your fingers in the hand vinegar and press each portion of rice into a cylinder shape. Put one of the cylinders in the middle of one piece of seaweed and spread it evenly over the sheet, leaving about ¾ inch bare.

4 Brush ¼ teaspoon wasabi down the middle of the rice and put a line of cucumber on top.

5 Roll it up following the method on pages 16–17, then make a second roll using the remaining ingredients.

6 The sushi can be wrapped in plastic and left like this until you are ready to cut and serve.

7 To serve, cut in half with a wet knife and trim off the end (optional—you may like to leave a "cockade" of cucumber sticking out of the end). Cut each half in 3 and arrange on a serving platter. Small dishes of soy sauce, pickled ginger, and wasabi paste are traditional accompaniments.

This simple little roll makes a colorful addition to a sushi plate. Try using a selection of different vegetables such as carrot, cucumber, radish, beet, and red, yellow, or orange bell peppers.

bright vegetable and thin omelet rolls

3 extra-large eggs

2 teaspoons Japanese soy sauce

2–3 teaspoons peanut oil

3 sheets nori seaweed, halved

½ recipe Vinegared Rice (page 11), divided into 6 portions

4 oz. mixed vegetables (see recipe introduction), very finely sliced

1 teaspoon wasabi paste (optional

HAND VINEGAR

¼ cup Japanese rice vinegar

1 cup water

a Japanese omelet pan or 8-inch skillet

MAKES 36 PIECES

1 Mix the hand vinegar ingredients in a small bowl and set aside.

2 Put the eggs and soy sauce in a bowl or small pitcher and beat well. Heat a film of oil in the omelet pan or skillet and pour in one-third of the beaten egg mixture. Swirl the egg around to cover the base of the pan and cook for about 1 minute until set. Carefully remove the omelet to a plate and cook the remaining egg mixture in 2 batches. Cut each omelet in half.

3 Put a sheet of nori, rough side up with the long edge towards you, on a sushi rolling mat. Dip your fingers in the hand vinegar and take 1 portion of the vinegared rice and a piece of omelet (trim the end of the omelet if it hangs over the end of the rice). Arrange a line of vegetables along the edge closest to you and smear a little wasabi, if using, in a line next to the vegetables.

4 Carefully roll up, brushing a little water along the edge of the nori to seal if necessary. Repeat to make 6 rolls, then slice each roll into 6 even pieces.

broiled tofu roll

6 oz. silken tofu

2 tablespoons Japanese soy sauce

1 tablespoon mirin (sweetened Japanese rice wine)

1 teaspoon sugar

3 sheets nori seaweed, halved (you need 5 pieces, so you will have ½ sheet left over)

1 tablespoon white sesame seeds, toasted in a dry skillet

1 tablespoon black sesame seeds

1 tablespoon oboro (dried pink fish flakes)

½ recipe Vinegared Rice (page 11), divided into 4 portions

1 teaspoon wasabi paste, plus extra to serve

HAND VINEGAR

¼ cup Japanese rice vinegar

1 cup water

a metal tray, lined with parchment paper

MAKES 24–32 PIECES

Silken tofu makes a moist, tender filling—sometimes firm tofu can be a bit tough. To make silken tofu a little firmer, put it in a bowl and cover it with boiling water before you start making the sushi.

1 Cut the tofu into ½-inch square strips and arrange in a shallow dish. Put the soy sauce, mirin, and sugar in a small bowl or small pitcher and mix well. Pour the mixture evenly over the tofu and set aside to marinate for 10 minutes.

2 Preheat the broiler. Put the tofu on a metal tray lined with parchment paper and broil for 2 minutes, turn the pieces over, brush with marinade. and broil for a further 2 minutes. Set aside to cool.

3 Cut ½ sheet of nori into tiny shreds (about ¹⁄₁₆ inch), put in a small bowl, and stir in the sesame seeds and oboro.

4 Mix the hand vinegar ingredients in a small bowl and set aside.

5 Spread a sheet of plastic wrap on the rolling mat and put ½ sheet of nori on top of that. Dip your fingers in the hand vinegar, take 1 portion of the vinegared rice. Sprinkle with one-fourth of the seed mixture, and press lightly into the rice.

6 Carefully lift the whole thing up and flip it over so the rice is face down on the plastic wrap. Arrange slices of broiled tofu along the long edge of the nori closest to you, smear with a little wasabi paste and carefully roll up. Repeat to make 4 rolls, then slice each roll into 6–8 pieces. Serve with extra wasabi and your choice of sushi accompaniments.

One simple ingredient can make a perfectly elegant filling for rolled sushi. Here fresh green asparagus is marinated in white miso.

miso-marinated asparagus roll

1 Snap off any tough ends from the asparagus and discard. Bring a large saucepan of water to a boil, add the asparagus, and simmer for 3–4 minutes until tender. Drain, rinse in plenty of cold water, then let cool.

2 If using medium asparagus, slice each piece in half lengthwise to give 24 pieces. Arrange all the asparagus in a shallow dish.

3 Put the white miso paste, mirin, and wasabi paste in a small bowl and mix well. Spread evenly over the asparagus and let marinate for 2–4 hours.

4 When ready to assemble the rolls, carefully scrape the marinade off the asparagus—it should be fairly clean, so the miso doesn't overwhelm the flavor.

5 Mix the hand vinegar ingredients in a small bowl and set aside.

6 Put 1 half-sheet of nori, rough side up with the long edge towards you, on a sushi rolling mat. Dip your fingers in the hand vinegar, take 1 portion of the vinegared rice and spread it out in a thin layer over the nori, leaving about ¾ inch bare on the far edge.

7 Put 4 pieces of the asparagus in a line along the middle of the rice. Lift the edge of the mat closest to you and start rolling up the sushi away from you, pressing in the filling with your fingers as you roll. You may need a little water along the far edge to seal it. Repeat to make 6 rolls in all. Using a clean, wet knife, slice each roll in half, then each half into 3, giving 6 even pieces per roll. Serve.

24 small or 12 medium asparagus spears

3 oz. white miso paste

2 teaspoons mirin (sweetened Japanese rice wine)

1 teaspoon wasabi paste

3 sheets nori seaweed, halved

½ recipe Vinegared Rice (page 11), divided into 6 portions

HAND VINEGAR

¼ cup Japanese rice vinegar

1 cup water

MAKES 36 PIECES

Mushrooms are a popular Japanese vegetable. Most supermarkets carry fresh shiitakes, and many may have enokis, like little clumps of white nails with tiny caps, and their bigger brothers, the hon-shigiri, with brown "berets" on their heads. If unavailable, use oyster and button mushrooms.

mushroom omelet sushi roll

4 oz. fresh shiitake mushrooms, about 12, stalks removed

4 oz. oyster mushrooms

2 oz. enoki mushrooms, roots trimmed

3 teaspoons peanut oil

1 tablespoon Japanese soy sauce

1 tablespoon mirin (sweetened Japanese rice wine)

2 eggs

¼ teaspoon sea salt

4 sheets nori seaweed

½ recipe Vinegared Rice (page 11), divided into 4 portions

HAND VINEGAR

¼ cup Japanese rice vinegar

1 cup water

a Japanese omelet pan or 10-inch skillet, preferably nonstick

MAKES 24–32 PIECES

1 Slice the shiitake and oyster mushrooms into ½-inch slices. Separate the enoki mushrooms into bunches of two or three.

2 Heat 2 teaspoons of the oil in a large skillet and sauté the shiitake and oyster mushrooms for 2 minutes, add the enoki and stir-fry for 1½ minutes. Add the soy sauce and mirin and toss to coat. Remove from the heat and let cool. Divide into 4 portions.

3 Put the eggs and salt in a bowl and beat well. Heat ½ teaspoon of the oil in the pan or skillet. Slowly pour in half of the egg, tipping the pan to get an even coating. Cook for about 1 minute until set, roll up, remove from the pan, and let cool. Repeat with the remaining egg to make a second omelet. Slice the two rolled omelets in half lengthwise.

4 Mix the hand vinegar ingredients in a small bowl and set aside.

5 Put 1 sheet of nori, rough side up with the long edge towards you, on a sushi rolling mat. Dip your fingers in the hand vinegar, take 1 portion of the vinegared rice and spread it out in a thin layer over the nori, leaving about 1 inch bare at the far edge. Put a strip of omelet down the middle and top with 1 portion of the mushrooms. Carefully roll up the nori in the mat, pressing the ingredients into the roll as you go. Wet the bare edge of nori and finish rolling to seal. Repeat to make 4 rolls.

6 Slice each roll into 6–8 pieces and serve.

inside-out avocado rolls
with chives and cashews

Rolling inside-out sushi may seem a bit hard, but it is actually very easy because the rice on the outside molds into shape so well, and it also looks spectacular.

2 small or 1 large ripe avocado

2 teaspoons lemon juice

2 tablespoons Japanese mayonnaise

¼ teaspoon sea salt

1 teaspoon wasabi paste (optional)

3 oz. cashews, pan-toasted (roasted salted cashews work well)

a small bunch of chives

2 sheets nori seaweed, halved

½ recipe Vinegared Rice (page 11), divided into 4 portions

HAND VINEGAR

¼ cup Japanese rice vinegar

1 cup water

MAKES 24 PIECES

1 Peel the avocado and cut the flesh into small chunks. Put in a bowl with the lemon juice, mayonnaise, salt, and wasabi, if using. Toss and mash slightly, but not until mushy! Divide into 4 portions.

2 Chop the cashews very finely and put in a bowl. Chop the chives very finely and mix with the cashews. Divide into 4 portions.

3 Mix the hand vinegar ingredients in a small bowl and set aside.

4 Put a sheet of plastic wrap on the rolling mat. Put ½ sheet of nori on top, rough side up with the long edge towards you. Dip your fingers in the hand vinegar, take 1 portion of the vinegared rice and spread it out in a thin layer over the nori, leaving about ¾ inch bare on the far edge.

5 Sprinkle 1 portion of the nut and chive mixture on top of the rice and press it in gently with your fingers.

6 Carefully lift the whole thing up and flip it over so the rice is face down on the plastic wrap. Remove the sushi mat. Put 1 portion of the avocado in a line along the long edge of the nori closest to you. Carefully roll it up, then cut in half, then each half into 3, giving 6 pieces. Repeat to make 4 rolls, giving 24 pieces.

pickled zucchini roll
with beet sashimi

A thinly sliced ribbon of zucchini makes a stunning alternative to nori on the outside of a sushi roll. It is easiest to cut the zucchini and beet with a mandoline—the plastic Japanese ones are marvelous and inexpensive—but if you don't have one you can use a good sharp peeler or knife and a steady hand.

1 To make the pickling mixture, put the vinegar, sugar, and mirin in a small saucepan and bring to a boil, stirring. Reduce to a simmer and cook for 5 minutes. Remove from the heat and let cool.

2 Thinly slice the zucchini and/or squash lengthwise, discarding the first and last couple of pieces (they will be too narrow). Arrange the slices flat in a shallow dish or container and pour the pickling mixture over the top. Set aside for 4 hours or overnight.

3 When ready to assemble the sushi, peel the raw beets and slice them carefully, as thinly as possible.

4 Put the wasabi and mayonnaise in a small bowl and mix well.

5 Mix the hand vinegar ingredients in a small bowl and set aside.

6 Dip your fingers in the hand vinegar, divide the seasoned rice into 18 walnut-size portions and shape each piece into a flattened ball. Wrap a ribbon of pickled zucchini around the outside of each piece, then top with a dab of wasabi mayonnaise and a couple of thin slivers of raw beet.

7 To make the dipping sauce, mix the soy sauce and sake together and serve in a small bowl beside the sushi.

3 medium zucchini or yellow squash, or both

1–2 very small beets or 5–6 baby beets, uncooked

1 teaspoon wasabi paste

1½ tablespoons Japanese mayonnaise

½ recipe Vinegared Rice (page 11)

PICKLING MIXTURE

1 cup Japanese rice vinegar

⅓ cup sugar

2 tablespoons mirin (sweetened Japanese rice wine)

HAND VINEGAR

¼ cup Japanese rice vinegar

1 cup water

DIPPING SAUCE

2 tablespoons Japanese mild soy sauce

1 tablespoon sake

MAKES 18 PIECES

PRESSED SUSHI

Battera, a speciality from Osaka, is one of the most popular sushi in Japan. It is made in a container or molded into a log with a sushi mat and cut into small pieces. In restaurants and stores it often comes wrapped in a transparent sheet of kombu (dried kelp).

mackerel sushi pieces battera

10 oz. very fresh mackerel fillet

sea salt

3–4 tablespoons Japanese rice vinegar

½ recipe Vinegared Rice (page 11)

HAND VINEGAR

2 tablespoons rice vinegar

½ cup water

TO SERVE

Pickled Ginger (page 123)

Japanese soy sauce

a wooden mold or rectangular plastic container, 7 x 4½ x 2 inches

MAKES 1 BATTERA: 16 PIECES

1 Start the preparation for this dish a few hours before cooking the rice. Take a dish larger than the fish fillets and cover with a thick layer of salt. Put the mackerel fillets, flesh side down, on top of the salt and cover completely with more salt. Set aside for 3–4 hours. Remove the mackerel and rub off the salt with damp paper towels. Carefully remove all the bones with tweezers, then put into a dish and pour the rice vinegar over the fillets. Leave to marinate for 30 minutes.

2 Mix the hand vinegar ingredients in a small bowl and set aside.

3 Using your fingers, carefully remove the transparent skin from each fillet, starting at the tail end. Put the fillets, skin side down, on a cutting board and slice off the highest part from the center of the flesh so the fillets will be fairly flat. Keep the trimmings.

4 Line a wet wooden mold or rectangular container with a large piece of plastic wrap.

5 Put a fillet, skin side down, in the mold or container. Fill the gaps with the other fillet and trimmings. Dip your fingers in the hand vinegar, then press the cooked rice down firmly on top of the fish. Put the wet wooden lid on top, or fold in the plastic and put a piece of cardboard and a weight on top.

6 You can leave it in a cool place for a few hours. When ready to serve, remove from the container and unwrap any plastic. Take a very sharp knife and wipe it with a vinegar-soaked cloth or piece of paper towel. Cut the block of sushi in 4 lengthwise, then in 4 crosswise, making 16 pieces.

7 Arrange on a plate, and serve with pickled ginger and a little soy sauce in small individual dishes.

masu-zushi smoked fish sushi

Pressed sushi (*oshi-zushi*) like this, or log sushi (*bo-zushi*), will keep for up to 36 hours—as a result, they are the best-selling items at all Japanese airports. Travelers buy them for Japanese friends living abroad as a reminder of the true taste of Japan. They are easy to make and can be made the day before.

1 Mix the hand vinegar ingredients in a small bowl and set aside.

2 Lay the smoked trout or salmon slices evenly in the bottom of a wet wooden mold. Alternatively, use a rectangular container lined with a piece of plastic wrap large enough for the edges to hang out of the container.

3 Wet your hands in the hand vinegar, transfer the vinegared rice into the mold and press it firmly and evenly into the mold. Put the wet wooden lid on top. If using a plastic container, fold in the plastic wrap to cover the rice and top with a piece of cardboard just big enough to cover the rice, and put a weight on top for 2–3 hours or overnight.

4 When ready to serve, remove from the container and unwrap any plastic. Take a very sharp knife and wipe it with a cloth soaked in vinegar or a piece of paper towel. Cut the sushi into 4 lengthwise, then in 4 crosswise, making 16 pieces.

5 Arrange on a large serving plate. Put a fan-shaped piece of lemon on top. Serve with pickled ginger and a little Japanese soy sauce.

½ recipe Vinegared Rice (page 11)

HAND VINEGAR

2 tablespoons Japanese rice vinegar

½ cup water

TOPPINGS

6 oz. smoked trout or smoked salmon, thickly sliced

2 slices lemon, cut into 16 fan-shaped pieces

TO SERVE

Pickled Ginger (page 123)

Japanese soy sauce

a wooden mold or rectangular plastic container, 7 x 4½ x 2 inches

MAKES 1 BLOCK: 16 PIECES

stars, hearts, and flowers

1 Put the fish in a saucepan, add just enough boiling water to cover, and simmer until well-cooked. Drain, then carefully remove all the small bones. Pat dry with paper towels and return to the dry saucepan. Using a fork, crush into fine flakes. Add the sugar and a pinch of salt, then cook over a low heat, continuously stirring with a fork, for about 2 minutes, or until the fish is very dry and flaky. If using red food coloring, dilute 1 drop with 1 tablespoon water, then stir quickly through the fish to spread the color evenly. Remove from the heat and let cool. (Alternatively, use fresh salmon cooked to flakes in the same way or crush canned cooked red salmon into flakes.)

2 Bring a small saucepan of lightly salted water to a boil, add the peas, and cook for 5 minutes or until soft. Drain and pat dry with paper towels. Crush with a mortar and pestle or in a food processor to form a smooth green paste. Stir in the sugar and a pinch of salt.

3 Lightly oil a small saucepan and set over moderate heat. Put the eggs, milk, and sugar in a bowl, mix, then pour into the pan. Quickly stir with a fork to make soft scrambled eggs. Remove from the heat and let cool.

4 Divide the vinegared rice into three. To make the cherry blossom sushi, put 1 tablespoon of the pink fish flakes in the bottom of a small heart-shaped mold and press 1 tablespoon rice on top. Turn out onto a plate, fish side up. Repeat until all the pink flakes and a third of the rice are used. Using a second mold, repeat using the green pea paste and another third of the rice. Using a third mold, repeat using the scrambled eggs with the remaining third of the rice. If using grilled fresh salmon, use a fourth mold.

5 Arrange cherry blossom, flower, star, and spring green sushi on a large serving plate.

½ recipe Vinegared Rice (page 11)

CHERRY BLOSSOM SUSHI

4 oz. cod or haddock fillet, skinned

2 tablespoons sugar

sea salt

red food coloring*

SPRING GREEN SUSHI

1 cup frozen peas

2 teaspoons sugar

sea salt

GOLDEN STAR SUSHI

2 eggs, beaten

1 tablespoon milk

1 tablespoon sugar

oil, for cooking

star, daisy, and heart-shaped sushi molds, or cookie cutters

MAKES 18–20 PIECES

*If you don't want to use the food coloring, use broiled fresh salmon, flaked, instead of the white fish and coloring.

eggcup sushi

Hand-molding of rice is rather a messy job and it's also difficult to make identical shapes and sizes. Using an eggcup as a mold is a simple solution. These sushi are very easy to make, pretty to serve, and delicious to eat.

5–6 smoked salmon slices, about 4 oz., halved to make 10–12 pieces

¼ recipe Vinegared Rice (page 11)

lemon or lime wedges, to serve

HAND VINEGAR

¼ cup Japanese rice vinegar

1 cup water

a small eggcup

MAKES 10–12 PIECES

1 Mix the hand vinegar ingredients in a small bowl and set aside.

2 Line an eggcup with plastic wrap so it hangs over the edge of the cup. Line the whole cup with a piece of smoked salmon, filling any gaps with small pieces of salmon. Put 1 tablespoon of vinegared rice in the cup and press down gently with your thumbs. Do not overfill. Trim the excess salmon from the rim. Lift up the plastic and turn out the molded sushi, upside down, onto a plate. Repeat to make 10 pieces.

3 Arrange on a platter, add lemon or lime wedges, and serve.

Variation Make soft scrambled eggs, using 2 eggs, 1 teaspoon sugar, and a pinch of salt. Let cool. Lay a piece of plastic in the eggcup. Put 1 teaspoon of the scrambled eggs on the bottom. Gently press to make a firm base—the egg should come about half way up the side of the cup. Put 1 tablespoon of vinegared rice on top of the egg and again gently press down with your thumbs. Do not overfill. Using the plastic, turn out the molded sushi, upside down, onto a plate. Repeat this process for the remainder of the egg and rice. Serve with a tiny bit of red caviar on top.

BAGS, BOWLS, AND BOXES

Gomoku-zushi means "5-kinds sushi" and usually has 5–8 ingredients. It is a popular luncheon dish.

lunchbox sushi mixture

1 recipe Vinegared Rice
(page 11)

TOPPINGS

3–4 dried shiitake mushrooms

⅓ cup sugar

3 tablespoons Japanese
soy sauce

½ carrot, finely sliced
into 1-inch strips

1 cup chicken stock or water

1 tablespoon sake

2 oz. green beans, trimmed

½ small lotus root (renkon)
(optional)

¾ cup Japanese rice vinegar

2 eggs, beaten

salt

sunflower oil, for cooking

SERVES 4–6

1 Soak the shiitakes in warm water for 30 minutes. Drain, retaining the soaking liquid. Remove and discard the stems, then thinly slice the caps. Put in a small saucepan, cover with ½ cup soaking liquid, 2 tablespoons sugar, and 2 tablespoons soy sauce. Simmer for 10 minutes or until most of the liquid disappears. Transfer to a bowl and let cool.

2 Put the finely sliced carrot in the saucepan with water to cover. Bring to a boil, then drain in a colander. Put the chicken stock or water in the saucepan, add the remaining soy sauce and sake, bring to a boil, add the carrot, and cook for 3–4 minutes. Transfer to a bowl and let cool.

3 Add some lightly salted water to the saucepan, bring to a boil, add the beans and boil for 2 minutes until just soft. Drain and cool under running water. Pat dry with paper towels and slice diagonally into 2-inch long shreds.

4 Peel the lotus root, if using, and slice into thin rings. Bring a small saucepan of water to a boil, add 1 tablespoon rice vinegar and the lotus root, and boil until just soft. Drain and transfer to a mixing bowl. Put the remaining rice vinegar in the saucepan, add the remaining sugar and 2 teaspoons salt, bring to a boil, and stir until dissolved. Remove from the heat, add to the lotus root, and let marinate for 15–20 minutes.

5 Beat the eggs with a pinch of salt. Heat an 8-inch skillet, brush with sunflower oil, add the egg, and cook until just set. Transfer the egg pancake to a cutting board and cut into fine shreds, 2 inches long.

6 Put the rice in a bowl and fold in all the ingredients except the egg shreds and a few of the beans. Transfer to bowls or lunchboxes, top with the egg shreds and beans, and serve.

Fukusa is an elaborate napkin used for the traditional Japanese tea ceremony. It is folded in various ways and is an important part of the classic performance. It has lent its name to this folded pancake sushi.

omelet package sushi
fukusa-zushi

½ recipe Vinegared Rice (page 11)

10 eggs, beaten

2 tablespoons sugar

½ teaspoon sea salt

1 teaspoon cornstarch blended with 1 teaspoon water

2 tablespoons sesame seeds (black or white)

2 oz. canned anchovies, finely chopped

1 bunch of mizuna (optional)

sunflower oil, for cooking

HAND VINEGAR

¼ cup Japanese rice vinegar

1 cup water

TO SERVE

Pickled Ginger (page 123)

Japanese soy sauce

MAKES 8 PACKAGES

1 Put the eggs in a large mixing bowl and lightly beat with a fork. Strain through a sieve into another bowl. Add the sugar, salt, and blended cornstarch and mix well until dissolved. Do not whip.

2 Heat an 8-inch skillet, add a little oil, and spread over the base with a paper towel. Add 1 small ladle of the egg mixture and spread evenly over the base by tilting the skillet. Cook over a low heat for about 30 seconds on each side until it becomes firm but not browned. Transfer to a plate and let cool. Repeat to make 8 egg pancakes.

3 Put the sesame seeds in a small saucepan and toss over a moderate heat until they start to pop. Remove from the heat and coarsely crush with a mortar and pestle.

4 Mix the hand vinegar ingredients in a small bowl and set aside.

5 While the rice is still warm, fold in the chopped anchovy fillets and crushed sesame seeds. Dip your hands in the hand vinegar, then divide the rice mixture into 8 balls.

6 Put an egg pancake on a board and put a rice ball in the center. Fold the front of the pancake over the rice, then fold over the 2 sides, then the far side, like an envelope. Tuck the edges into the sides. Repeat to make 8 parcels. Alternatively, fold into a money bag, as shown (inset).

7 If using mitzuna to tie the parcels, soak the stems in boiling water for about 30 seconds, using 2 pieces per parcel. Serve with pickled ginger and soy sauce.

An *inari* is a shrine dedicated to agriculture and the fox is regarded as the envoy of the god. People used to offer *abura-age* (fried tofu) to the fox; hence this special name. This sushi makes an ideal picnic lunch and children's snack.

tofu bags inari-zushi

½ recipe Vinegared Rice (page 11)

3 fresh Japanese fried tofu (abura-age)

¾ cup chicken stock

3 tablespoons sugar

2 tablespoons mirin (sweetened Japanese rice wine) or sweet sherry

2 tablespoons Japanese soy sauce

2 dried shiitake mushrooms

2 inches carrot, finely chopped

1 tablespoon sake (optional)

HAND VINEGAR

¼ cup Japanese rice vinegar

1 cup water

TO SERVE

Pickled Ginger (page 123)

Japanese soy sauce

MAKES 6 TOFU BAGS

1 Put the fried tofu (abura-age) on a cutting board and roll each one with a rolling pin. This separates the thin layers inside the tofu, making a bag. Put the tofu in a mixing bowl, pour over boiling water, then drain—this will reduce the oiliness.

2 Cut each piece in half and carefully open each piece from the cut side (if not opened already), to make a bag.

3 Put the chicken stock or water in a saucepan, add 2 tablespoons of the sugar, and bring to a boil. Add the tofu bags, cook for 3 minutes on moderate heat, then add 1 tablespoon mirin and 1 tablespoon soy sauce. Simmer over low heat for about 10 minutes until all the liquid disappears. Remove from the heat and transfer to a plate.

4 Meanwhile, soak the dried shiitakes in a bowl of warm water for at least 30 minutes, then drain, reserving the liquid. Cut off the stems and finely chop the caps. Pour ¼ cup of the soaking liquid into a saucepan, add the remaining sugar, mirin, soy sauce, and sake, if using, and bring to a boil. Add the carrot and shiitakes and simmer for 3–4 minutes until almost all the liquid is absorbed. Remove from the heat and let cool.

5 Mix the hand vinegar ingredients in a small bowl and set aside.

6 While the rice is still warm, fold in the cooked carrot and shiitakes. Dip your hands in the hand vinegar and divide the rice mixture into 6 balls. Squeeze out excess juice from the tofu bags and open with your fingers. Stuff a ball of rice into each bag and fold in the edge (optional).

7 Arrange the bags on a serving plate and serve with pickled ginger and soy sauce.

stuffed squid sushi ika-zushi

Meat is rarely used in sushi but this sweet, dry-cooked ground meat goes well with vinegared rice. It can be eaten as it is, or use it as a filling for squid and serve as an unusual party canapé. If you don't like to use meat, just use the squid flaps and tentacles in the sumeshi mixture, but reduce the cooking juice accordingly.

1 Mix the hand vinegar ingredients in a small bowl and set aside.

2 Peel the outer skin off the squid. It comes off easily if you hold the two flaps together and peel down the body. Put the 2 main bodies in a saucepan, add 1 tablespoon sake, cover with boiling water, and simmer for 1–2 minutes. Do not overcook. Drain, rub the surface with a damp cloth to remove any marks, then sprinkle with the rice vinegar all over to retain the whiteness. Chop the flaps and tentacles.

3 Put the remaining sake, the sugar, mirin, and soy sauce in a saucepan, mix, and bring to a boil over moderate heat. Add the ground chicken or beef, the chopped squid flaps and tentacles, and the chopped ginger, then stir vigorously with a fork until the meat turns white. Using a slotted spoon, transfer the cooked meat to another bowl, leaving the juice in the saucepan. Boil the juice over high heat for 1–2 minutes until thickened. Stir the meat back into the saucepan to absorb the juice and remove from heat.

4 Make the vinegared rice following the method on page 11 and, while still warm, fold in the dry-cooked meat. Tightly fill each squid body with half the rice mixture and, using a sharp knife, slice crosswise into 5–6 pieces.

5 Arrange on plates and serve with pickled ginger.

2 medium squid, cleaned

3 tablespoons sake

2–3 tablespoons Japanese rice vinegar

2 tablespoons sugar

1 tablespoon mirin (sweetened Japanese rice wine) or sweet sherry

2 tablespoons Japanese soy sauce

2 oz. ground chicken or beef

1 inch fresh ginger, peeled and finely chopped

⅔ recipe Vinegared Rice (page 11)

Pickled Ginger (page 123), to serve

HAND VINEGAR

¼ cup Japanese rice vinegar

1 cup water

MAKES 10–12 PIECES

sushi in a bowl edomae chirashi-zushi

A bowl of sushi with sashimi on top is a favorite in Tokyo. You can use just one ingredient like tuna, or the assorted sashimi normally used in restaurants.

1 Make the vinegared rice (sumeshi) following the method on page 11.

2 Bring a saucepan of lightly salted water to a boil, add the shrimp and poach for 1–2 minutes until just pink. Remove with a slotted spoon, cool under running water, then pat dry with paper towels.

3 Return the pan of water to a boil, add the octopus tentacle, and cook for 7–8 minutes. Drain and cool under running water. Pat dry with paper towels and slice diagonally into thin disks.

4 Cut the fish into 4 slices each.

5 Put the squid, skin side up, on a cutting board and make very fine slits two-thirds of the way through the thickness, first lengthwise, then crosswise. Put in a bowl, pour over boiling water, and drain. As the squid curls up, the slits open to form a flower. Immediately plunge into cold water. Pat dry with paper towels and cut into 4 bite size pieces.

6 Soak the shiitakes in warm water for 30 minutes and drain, retaining the soaking liquid. Cut off the stems and put in a saucepan with the sugar, mirin, and a pinch of salt. Cover with some of the soaking liquid, stir, then bring to a boil and simmer for 4–5 minutes until most of the liquid disappears. Let cool in the liquid.

7 Cut 2 green slices off the cucumber, 2 inches wide. Make fine slits lengthwise, leaving ½ inch intact on one side. Open up the slits to make 2 cucumber fans.

8 Divide the rice between 2 bowls and arrange the seafood over the rice and top with a cucumber fan and a pile of pink pickled ginger. Serve on small individual plates with a tiny heap of wasabi and a little pitcher of soy sauce.

½ recipe Vinegared Rice (page 11)

SASHIMI: YOUR CHOICE OF

2 uncooked medium shrimp, peeled but with tail fins intact

1 octopus tentacle

4 oz. fresh tuna and/or salmon

1 grouper or bass fillet, about 3 oz.

1 small squid, cleaned and skinned

2 large dried shiitake mushrooms

1 teaspoon sugar

1 teaspoon mirin (sweetened Japanese rice wine)

sea salt

TO SERVE

2 inches cucumber

Pickled Ginger (page 123)

wasabi paste

Japanese soy sauce

SERVES 2

tub of spring sushi

1 recipe Vinegared Rice
(page 11)

RADISH PETALS

4–5 radishes, trimmed

2 tablespoons Japanese
rice vinegar

2 tablespoons sugar

EGG PETALS

1 egg, beaten

¼ teaspoon cornstarch mixed
with a little water

sunflower oil, for cooking

YOUR CHOICE OF

5 dried shiitake mushrooms

⅓ cup sugar

2½ tablespoons mirin
(sweetened Japanese
rice wine)

1 teaspoon Japanese
soy sauce

¼ cup chicken stock

½ carrot, sliced into 1-inch
matchsticks

1 oz. snowpeas, trimmed

3 oz. cod fillet

1 tablespoon sake

red food coloring (optional)

8 oz. small shrimp, peeled and
lightly cooked

3 tablespoons white sesame
seeds, lightly toasted
in a dry skillet

sea salt

*flower cutters or a small sharp
knife*

SERVES 4–6

1 Make the vinegared rice (sumeshi) following the method on page 11.

2 Cut a wedge out of each radish, then slice each radish crosswise to form 5–6 petal shapes. Put the rice vinegar and sugar in a bowl and stir well until sugar has dissolved. Add the radish slices and marinate for a few hours or overnight. The red color dissolves into the vinegar, making the slices cherry pink.

3 Mix the egg in a bowl with a pinch of salt and the blended cornstarch. Heat a small skillet, brush with sunflower oil, add the egg mixture, and cook until set. Using molds or a small knife, cut out small shapes from the egg pancake such as hearts or petals.

4 Soak the shiitakes in warm water for 30 minutes, then drain, retaining the soaking liquid. Discard the stems and thinly slice the caps crosswise. Put the shiitake slices, ½ cup from the soaking liquid, and 2 tablespoons of the sugar in a saucepan, bring to a boil, and cook for 3–4 minutes. Add the mirin and soy sauce, then simmer until the liquid disappears.

5 Put the chicken stock in a saucepan, add ½ teaspoon of the sugar, a pinch of salt, and the carrot. Bring to a boil and cook for 2–3 minutes until just soft. Let cool in the juice.

6 Blanch the snowpeas in lightly salted water. Slice diagonally into diamonds.

7 Bring a saucepan of water to a boil, add the cod, simmer for 3–4 minutes, then drain. Carefully remove the skin and all the bones. Return to a dry saucepan, add the sake, the remaining sugar, and a pinch of salt. Finely flake over a low heat, using a fork. If using red coloring, dilute it in a little water, then quickly stir to make the fish flakes light pink.

8 While the rice is still warm, fold in the shiitakes, carrot matchsticks, flaked fish, shrimp, and sesame seeds. Top with the radish and egg "petals" and serve.

SASHIMI

Absolutely fresh fish is vital for sashimi. Buy from a retailer that specifies "sashimi-grade" or "sushi-grade" fish. Wherever possible, instead of buying ready-cut fillets, buy whole fish and ask the fishmonger to fillet it for you. With big fish, such as tuna or salmon, fillets are fine.

classic sashimi

1 fillet white fish such as fluke, flounder, or sole

1 slice of lemon, cut into 8 fan-shaped wedges

2 small fresh mackerel fillets

salt

Japanese rice vinegar

6 oz. tuna

6 oz. salmon fillet

1 small squid, cleaned and skinned

2 inches large daikon (white radish), peeled

ice water

4 shiso leaves (optional)

TO SERVE

4 teaspoons wasabi paste

Japanese soy sauce

SERVES 4

1 To skin the fillets, put them on a cutting board, skin side down. Hold down the skin of the tail with your fingers, then run the blade along the skin, separating the flesh. Cut the whole fillet lengthwise along the center line. Insert the blade diagonally against the cutting board and slice each fillet crosswise into 8 pieces, ½-inch thick. Make a slit in each piece and insert a fan-shaped piece of lemon.

2 Salt and vinegar the mackerel following the method on page 28. Slice the fillets into ½-inch pieces, as above.

3 Slice the tuna and salmon into 8 pieces, 2 x 1 x ½ inch thick.

4 Cut the squid into 8 pieces and finely slice each piece lengthwise, leaving the pieces attached at one end.

5 Using a mandoline or sharp knife, finely shred the daikon. Put the shreds in a bowl of ice water for about 30 minutes to make them crisp. Drain and pat dry with paper towels.

6 To serve, put a mound of daikon shreds, a small mound of wasabi, and a shiso leaf, if using, on each plate. Add 2 slices of each fish and serve with a small dish of Japanese soy sauce.

seared tuna sashimi salad

It may take time to get used to the idea of eating completely raw fish, but lightly blanched or seared fillet with salad is a good starting point. You can use other fish such as salmon.

8 oz. fresh tuna or swordfish, skinned

ice water

green salad leaves

a small clump of enoki mushrooms, trimmed and separated

WASABI DRESSING

freshly squeezed juice of 1 lemon

2 teaspoons wasabi paste

1½ tablespoons Japanese soy sauce

SERVES 4

1 Cook the tuna or swordfish on a stove-top grill pan at a high heat for about 1 minute on each side until the surfaces are seared but the inside is still raw. Plunge into ice water. Drain and pat dry with paper towels. Slice into ⅛-inch thick pieces.

2 Mix the lemon juice, wasabi, and soy sauce in a small bowl and set aside.

3 Arrange the salad leaves and enoki mushrooms in the center of a large serving plate and arrange the seared fish over the leaves. Just before serving, pour the wasabi dressing over the top.

MISO SOUPS

A good dashi, or soup stock, is the basis for any great miso soup. A very simple version requires only kombu and water, but fresh and dried fish give an exceptional result. Packages of little dried fish are sold in Japanese and other Asian supermarkets. Many miso pastes come premixed with dashi, but the recipes in this book call for pure miso paste—so check the package. If you do have dashi included in your paste, replace the dashi quantity with water. Different qualities of miso paste will have different strengths, so adjust quantities according to taste.

dashi and combination
miso soup

2-inch piece of kombu (dried kelp)

1 tablespoon bonito flakes

COMBINATION MISO SOUP

2 tablespoons red miso paste

2 tablespoons white miso paste

MAKES 6 CUPS DASHI:
SOUP SERVES 4

1 To make the dashi, bring 3 quarts water to the boil, add the kombu and bonito, return almost to the boil but do not let boil. Turn off the heat and let stand for 10 minutes. Strain and use immediately, or cool and store in the refrigerator for up to 2 days, or freeze for up to 3 months.

2 To make the soup, put the red miso and white miso pastes in a small bowl. Add ¼ cup dashi and stir well.

3 Pour 1 quart dashi into a saucepan, bring to a boil, reduce to a simmer, and stir in the miso mixture. Return to simmering point, but do not boil. Serve in 4 small bowls. (Reserve the remaining dashi for another use.)

Miso pastes, widely used in Japanese soups, are made from soy beans, and so is the tofu in this soup. There are many flavors and varieties of miso, but there are three main categories, with cultures based on barley, rice, and soy beans. All three are easy to find, either in the Japanese section of larger supermarkets, in natural food stores, or by mail order.

japanese miso soup

1 Remove the tofu from its container and slide it carefully onto a small plate. Put another plate on top and set aside for 30 minutes to press out some of the liquid. You can put a very small food can on top if you wish, but nothing too heavy.

2 Put the wakame in a bowl of water and let soften. Cut out any stiff sections with kitchen shears and discard. Cut the wakame into 1-inch strips.

3 Put the dashi in a saucepan, bring almost to a boil, then reduce to a simmer. Set a fine-mesh sieve over the saucepan and add the miso. Using the back of a ladle, press the miso into the dashi and reduce the heat so the soup doesn't boil.

4 Add the wakame and simmer for 2 minutes.

5 Cut the tofu in half through its thickness. Cut into ½-inch cubes and drop into the soup (it is easier to do this if you hold the tofu cake in your palm and slice it carefully—it is very fragile). When the tofu floats to the surface, like ravioli, it is cooked. Carefully ladle into soup bowls, sprinkle the scallion over the top, and serve.

Note This is the traditional accompaniment to sushi and similar dishes. The soup is drunk at the end—eat the tofu and wakame with chopsticks, then pick up the bowl and sip. (The rim and foot of the traditional lacquer bowls are specially designed not to be heat conductors, so you won't burn yourself.)

1 tub silken tofu
1 quart Dashi (page 109)
2 oz. wakame (dried seaweed)*
3 tablespoons dark miso paste
1 tablespoon white miso paste
1 scallion, chopped

SERVES 4

*Japanese ingredients are now widely available, especially in natural food stores, but if you can't find wakame, a few sprigs of watercress would taste delicious.

The more mellow flavors of white miso make a perfect drink to serve with sushi rolls—the delicious and delicate taste of this soup will not overpower even the most subtle of sushi.

white miso soup
with wakame, tofu, and lettuce

a pinch of wakame
(dried seaweed)

1 quart dashi stock

¼ cup white miso paste

4 oz. silken tofu,
cut into ¼-inch cubes

¼ iceberg or other crisp
lettuce, finely sliced (optional)

SERVES 4

1 Soak the wakame in a bowl of hot water for 15 minutes, then drain.

2 Pour the dashi stock in a saucepan, bring to a boil, then reduce to simmering. Mix the miso paste in a bowl with a few tablespoons of the dashi to loosen it, then stir it into the simmering stock. Add the tofu and wakame and cook in the soup for 1 minute.

3 Divide the lettuce, if using, between 4 bowls, ladle the hot soup over the top, then serve.

red miso soup
with pork and noodles

This heartier version of miso soup can be served before heavier meat- or poultry-based sushi rolls or after delicate fish or vegetarian rolls. It can also be beefed up with stir-fried vegetables as a great big bowl of soup for two.

8 oz. soba
(buckwheat) noodles

1 quart Dashi (page 109)

1 small leek, finely sliced

3 tablespoons red miso paste

4 oz. roast pork, thinly sliced

SERVES 4

1 Fill a large saucepan three-fourths full of water and bring to a boil. Add the soba and return to a boil. Add 1 cup of cold water and bring to a boil again. Boil for 3 minutes, drain, rinse in cold water, and drain again.

2 Pour the dashi stock in a saucepan and bring to a boil. Add the leeks and reduce to a simmer. Mix the miso paste in a bowl with a few tablespoons of the dashi to loosen it, then stir it into the simmering stock.

3 Divide the noodles and slices of roast pork between 4 bowls, ladle over the hot soup, then serve.

You need only about one-third of this batter for this recipe, but half an egg seems difficult to work with, so use the rest of the batter for tempura vegetables or shrimp. Alternatively, you could use the pressed croutons sold in Japanese stores.

red miso soup with scallions and crisp tempura croutons

1 quart Dashi (page 109)
3 tablespoons red miso paste
2 scallions, finely sliced

TEMPURA CROUTONS
1 egg, separated
1 tablespoon lemon juice
⅔ cup ice water
⅛ cup all-purpose flour
peanut or safflower oil, for frying

SERVES 4

1 To make the batter, put the egg yolk, lemon juice, and ice water in a bowl. Whisk gently, then whisk in the flour to form a smooth batter. Do not overmix.

2 Whisk the egg white in a second bowl until stiff but not dry, then fold into the batter.

3 To cook the croutons, fill a large wok or saucepan one-third full of oil and heat to 340°F, or until a small cube of bread turns golden in 30 seconds.

4 Carefully drop teaspoons of the batter into the oil and cook for 30 seconds until crispy. Scoop out and drain on paper towels.

5 Pour the dashi into a saucepan, bring to a boil, then reduce to a simmer. Mix the miso paste with a few tablespoons of the dashi to loosen it, then stir it into the simmering stock. Divide the stock between 4 bowls, add the croutons and scallions, and serve.

There are three main kinds of Japanese soups: the miso soups with tofu and wakame served as a "drink" with sushi or sashimi; the big soups, such as New Year Soup; and these—clear dashi in which floats one to three beautiful ingredients, each a complement to the other.

clear japanese soup with shrimp, citrus, and pepper

4 shelled medium uncooked shrimp, tail on

4 thin strips of citrus peel, such as yuzu if available, or lemon, tied in a knot, or a slice of carrot or other vegetable, blanched

1 quart Dashi (page 109), hot but not boiling, or 1 quart hot water with dashi powder

4 leaves of Japanese herb, such as shiso, or a slice of scallion

furikake seasoning, Japanese seven-spice, or black pepper, to serve

SERVES 4

1 Cut each shrimp along the belly without cutting all the way through. Open it out flat. Make a small slit where the backbone would be if it were a fish. Thread the tail up and through the slit in the back, then fan out the tail fins.

2 Cut the citrus zest with a cannelle cutter or zester. Put the zest and shrimp in a bowl and cover with boiling water.

3 Put the hot dashi in 4 Japanese soup bowls, add 1 shrimp, a knot of zest, and a shiso leaf or a slice of carrot or scallion. Put on the lid, then serve with a small dish of furikake seasoning, Japanese seven-spice, or black pepper.

BASICS

This is the basic method for cooking Japanese omelet. It is a regular breakfast item as well as being used for sushi.

japanese omelet
tamago yaki

1 Using a fork, beat the eggs and egg yolk and strain through a sieve into a bowl. Add the sugar, soy sauce, and pinch of salt and stir well until the sugar has dissolved. Do not whisk or make bubbles.

2 Heat a Japanese omelet pan or skillet over moderate heat and add a little oil. Spread evenly over the base by tilting the pan, then wipe off any excess oil with paper towels, at the same time making sure the surface is absolutely smooth. Keep the oiled paper on a plate.

3 Lower the heat and pour one-third of the egg mixture evenly over the base by tilting the pan. If large air bubbles pop up immediately, the pan may be too hot—if so, remove the pan from the heat and put it back on when the egg starts to set.

4 Prick any air bubbles with a fork and, when the egg is about to set, using chopsticks or a fork, roll the egg layer 2–3 times from one side to the other. Oil the empty base of the pan with the oiled paper and push the rolled egg back to the other side.

5 Again using the oiled paper, brush the base of the pan, then pour half the remaining egg mixture evenly over the base by tilting the pan and lifting the egg roll so the egg mixture flows underneath.

6 When the egg starts to set, roll again, using the first roll as the core. Repeat this oiling and rolling using up the remaining egg mixture. Remove from the pan and let cool before cutting.

4 eggs

1 egg yolk

2½ tablespoons sugar

1 teaspoon Japanese soy sauce

sea salt

1–2 tablespoons sunflower oil

1 Japanese omelet pan or 8-inch nonstick skillet

MAKES 1 OMELET

mixed pickles

Other vegetables can be pickled and served with sushi alongside ginger. They look wonderfully colorful, adding a touch of drama to your sushi platter, making it appear very professional.

½ cucumber, about 4 inches long

1 carrot, about 3 oz.

3 oz. daikon radish, peeled, or 6 red radishes

¼ small green cabbage, about 6 oz.

6 garlic cloves, thinly sliced

1 tablespoon sea salt

½ lemon, sliced

1 cup Japanese vinegar

1 cup sugar

MAKES ABOUT 2 CUPS

1 Cut the cucumber in half lengthwise and scoop out the seeds. Slice the cucumber, carrot, and daikon into very thin strips.

2 Slice the cabbage into ½-inch strips. Put all the vegetables and garlic in a colander, sprinkle with salt, and toss well. Set aside for 30 minutes, then rinse thoroughly and top with the sliced lemon.

3 Put the rice vinegar and sugar in a saucepan with ¼ cup water. Bring to a boil, stirring until the sugar has dissolved. Boil for 5 minutes. Let cool, then pour over the vegetables and lemon. Cover and chill for at least 24 hours or until needed. Keeps for 1 month in the refrigerator.

pickled ginger gari

Pickled ginger is the traditional companion for sushi. The subtle flavoring of raw fish, delicate rice, and fresh vegetables can easily be overpowered by the lingering flavors of previous morsels. Ginger helps cleanse the palate, introducing a sharp freshness that stimulates the taste buds for the next delight.

1 Peel the ginger and slice it very finely with a mandoline or vegetable peeler. Put it in a large strainer or colander and sprinkle with salt. Set aside for 30 minutes, then rinse thoroughly.

2 Put the rice vinegar and sugar in a saucepan, add ¼ cup water, and bring to a boil, stirring until the sugar has dissolved. Boil for 5 minutes. Let cool, then pour over the ginger. If you would like it to be pink, like store-bought ginger, add the beet, radish, or food coloring. Cover and refrigerate for at least 24 hours or until needed.

6 oz. piece of fresh ginger

1 tablespoon sea salt

½ cup Japanese rice vinegar

½ cup plus 1 tablespoon sugar

1 slice fresh beet, 1 red radish, sliced, or a drop of red food coloring (optional)

MAKES ABOUT 1 CUP

wasabi paste

Most of the wasabi we buy in tubes is a mixture of horseradish and wasabi—or it can be just horseradish dyed green. If you buy wasabi paste from a Japanese market, you will have a selection of various qualities, and it is always best to buy the best.

Many Japanese cooks prefer to mix their own paste from silver-gray wasabi powder, sold in small cans, like paprika, believing that the flavor is stronger and sharper. The fresh roots are not widely available, even in Japan, but if you see them in a speciality food store, sold on a bed of ice, do try them. To experience the real flavor and rush of wasabi you can make your own paste from them. It is traditionally grated using a sharkskin grater, but a porcelain ginger grater or a fine Microplane® grater will also work. After grating, the heat in wasabi lasts for only about 10 minutes, so you must use it right away.

wasabi from powder

1 teaspoon wasabi powder

SERVES 1

1 Put the wasabi powder in a small bowl, such as an eggcup. Add 1 teaspoon water and mix with the end of a chopstick. Serve immediately.

fresh wasabi paste

1 fresh wasabi root

a wasabi grater or other fine grater

SERVES 6–8

1 Scrape or peel off the rough skin from the root. Using a circular motion, rub the wasabi gently against an abrasive grater onto a chopping board. Pound and chop the grated wasabi to a fine paste with a large knife or cleaver. Consume within 10 minutes.

Note To stop the wasabi discoloring for as long as possible, turn the little bowl upside down until serving—this will stop the air getting at it.

index

picture credits

Photography by Peter Cassidy (except for the following)
Key: a=above, b=below, r=right, l=left, c=center
Martin Brigdale: 5, 8l, 8br, 10-11, 12l inset, 24, 26
Alan Williams: 7, 8ar, 18, 21l, 28c, 30